CW00496341

GEORGE ROBERTS MP

*Further details of Poppyland Publishing titles can be found at*
**www.poppyland.co.uk**
*where clicking on the 'Support and Resources' button
will lead to pages specially compiled to support this book*

*Join us for more Norfolk and Suffolk stories and background at*
**www.facebook.com/poppylandpublishing**

# George Roberts MP

## A LIFE THAT 'DID DIFFERENT'

by
Frank Meeres

POPPYLAND PUBLISHING

First published 2019 by Poppyland Publishing, Lowestoft, NR32 3BB
www.poppyland.co.uk

ISBN 978 1 909796 43 0

Designed and typeset in 10.5 on 13.5 pt Gilgamesh by Poppyland Publishing

**Picture credits**

All the illustrations in the book are from he Norfolk Record Office, except the following:
Illustrations on pp 34, 41, from 'Daylight', a local radical publication
Illustration on p 94: *Eastern Daily Press*

# Contents

# Acknowledgements

The papers of George Roberts were deposited with the Norfolk Record Office. Listing these I came to realise what a fascinating man he was, and was inspired to look further into his story, hence this book. I am grateful to the Norfolk Record Office for permission to use images from the collection.

# Introduction

George Roberts is one of Norfolk's most fascinating characters. Born in Chedgrave in 1868, the son of a shoemaker, he became the first Labour party Member of Parliament in East Anglia. He rose to become the party's Chief Whip and was one of the very small number of Labour MPs to serve in wartime Governments under David Lloyd George. He rose to become a cabinet minister and a privy councillor, serving in vital roles as Minister of Labour and then as Minister of Food.

After the war, disillusioned with the Labour Party, he stood for Norwich as an Independent candidate - and won! He then finished his journey to the right, becoming a Conservative MP!

George Roberts was always fiercely independent, making his own mind up on the great issues of the day and speaking out: he was never afraid of offending anyone. A little man, he was a big figure in local and national life in the first quarter of the twentieth century. He deserves to be far better known. This book brings to life the dramatic story of 'Georgie' Roberts.

*George Roberts as a statesman and politician: a portrait from his personal archive. It is possibly from a number of photographs taken at Versailles in 1919.*

# I

# 'What Mr Roberts would do if he had the power': George Roberts and the beginnings of Labour

Throughout his political career, Roberts was to lay stress on his background as that of the farm labourer. This appears to have been a slight exaggeration on his part. His father and grandfather were actually craftsmen — village shoemakers. In any case the family moved into Norwich when he was very young, so he can have had no personal memory of growing up in rural poverty. However, he was quite correct to claim a humble status for his family: his father could not sign the registration entry of George's birth, making his mark instead.

Roberts was born in the Norfolk village of Chedgrave on 27 July 1868. His father was George Henry Roberts, butcher and shoemaker, his mother Ann, formerly Larkman, a housemaid in the neighbouring village of Hardley. The couple married in Chedgrave church on Christmas Day 1867. Roberts was therefore conceived out of wedlock. This was much more of a stigma at that time than it is today, although not an insuperable one: two leading Labour politicians who appear in this book, Keir Hardie and Ramsay MacDonald, were illegitimate. However, Roberts covered up his background by a simple lie, and one that was never exposed in his lifetime. He always gave his date of birth as 27 July 1869 and this is the date given in all his obituaries and articles of biography.[1]

Roberts was baptised at nearby Thurton on 15 May 1870.[2] His mother was again pregnant and gave birth to a girl, Rebecca, three months later. Soon after this, Roberts' father decided to set up as a shoemaker in Norwich. At the time of the 1871 census (April) the family were living in Armes Street, off the Dereham Road: Roberts was two, his sister just nine months old.[3]

In later life Roberts sometimes said that he was one of a family of eight or nine — by the age of twelve, he claimed, he was the sole survivor. This claim was most dramatically told in *Lloyd's Sunday News* in 1919: 'Just over fifty years ago a delicate boy was born in a rural labourer's cottage in the Norfolk village of Chedgrave. Seven brothers and sisters followed but all, except the first born, died in very early childhood. By the time the boy was twelve he was the only child left to his struggling parents, and he lived despite the doctor's prophecies that he must soon follow the other children to their churchyard resting place.'

Certainly Rebecca died in 1877 at the age of seven: she was buried in the common grave at the Earlham Road cemetery in Norwich just two days before Christmas.[4] By the time of the 1881 census the family were living at Eagle Walk in Heigham, and George Roberts was the only child in the family, when he was indeed twelve years old. There does not seem to be time for the births and deaths of seven other children, so Roberts was perhaps exercising poetic licence on this point. Apart from George and Rebecca, no other children of the family were baptised or buried in the 1870s in Thurton or the neighbouring villages of Chedgrave, Langley or Hardley, and there are no other family burials in the Earlham Road cemetery. In his marriage announcement in 1895, Roberts is described as 'only son of G. H. Roberts'. Perhaps the, admittedly tragic, death of a baby sister, became the subject of some political spin over the years.

There was some very bad housing in the centre of Norwich at this time, families crowded together in tenements grouped around a yard with often a single water pump and a single privy. From the 1820s onwards, new housing was going up in Lakenham, especially the Peafield estate: these houses may have been new but they were still pretty appalling. The school that Roberts attended served this area, but Eagle Walk is slightly further out of the city, separated from Peafield by the Norfolk and Norwich Hospital. Most of the houses in the Walk have gone but a few still survive, small but, in that key word of Victorian England, 'respectable'. The cottages were built in the 1850s, just before the days of mains water and sewerage: bringing up a family here cannot have been easy.

Roberts went to school at the time of a revolution in education. Before 1870 the only schools in Norwich for poor children were supplied by various charitable bodies. Most of these were tied in with either Anglican or Nonconformist churches in the city. However, in 1870 elected School Boards were set up with the avowed intention of providing elementary education for every child for the first time.

According to his own account, Roberts' parents were concerned for his health in the city, and he spent most of his early childhood at Loddon, very near his birthplace: presumably he was looked after by relatives, probably by his uncle Henry (his father's brother), who was also a shoemaker and lived at a part of Loddon known as Gravel Pits. Henry had several children, including one boy, Sylvanus, who was two years older than Roberts. Roberts said later that he went to the village school for a few years, and then came back to live with his parents

*Roberts as a child between two adults — Ernest Wild the Conservative candidate and Louis Tillett the Liberal candidate.*

in Norwich. However, although Sylvanus did attend the school from June 1869 to November 1871, there is no record in the admission register of George Henry Roberts having been admitted. Perhaps he attended occasionally and informally with his cousin, but was never formally admitted as a pupil. In a speech in Parliament in 1915, he said that, because of his poor health, he was sent to stay with relatives in the Norfolk countryside on several occasions and attended local village schools. Typically, he could not resist asserting his own cleverness: on one such occasion he shared a bedroom with a local lad who was very keen on botany and had a book on the subject. Roberts was able to help him with the longer words in the book!

Roberts certainly went to the nearest elementary school, St Stephen's school in St Stephen's Square. This was a National school, built in 1865 to serve the many children in this rapidly-expanding part of the city. The school records survive, and, at last we are on firm ground. His uncle also moved into Norwich, with his family, living at Grove Place. Sylvanus was admitted to St Stephen's school, in January 1873, working through the first four standards (grades) and leaving in

1879 at the age of thirteen. George Henry Roberts followed him, being admitted to the school in April 1874, when he was five years nine months old (so any school days at Loddon or elsewhere must have been in the Infants' class).

The school had very few resources. A report of March 1875, while Roberts was a young pupil, said that 'the supply of Reading Books is quite insufficient and the Desks are very bad. The offices need attention'. Staffing was poor as well 'E J Walker and M Lee have passed an unsatisfactory examination. Should they be required to complete the Staff and fail to the same extent next year the Grant will have to be reduced by £20 and thenceforth by £40 for every year at the end of which a similar Failure is repeated'. By November the situation had improved and the threat to cut the grant was not repeated. This report said 'the year's work has been difficult and there is some improvement, but both discipline and instruction in the School are below the proper standard'. Standards appear to have improved during the years in which Roberts was a pupil, but there were still problems. In 1880 the head teacher noted high levels of absenteeism, and also of noise — not from the pupils but from the pupil-teachers! Elizabeth Grix, the 5th year pupil-teacher was a particular offender: perhaps she passed this trait on to the pupil who was to become the school's most distinguished old-boy![5]

Roberts recalled much later that he was 'a small delicate child whom his parents had little hope of rearing to manhood'. However, he did well at school passing through all six standards between 1875 and 1880. He became a monitor at the age of eleven, thus earning a few pence a week. Some thirty-five years later he recalled his schooldays in a speech in Parliament:

> Unfortunately the conditions and the position in which I was brought up did not enable my parents to place me in a high-class school. I had to attend a non-provided school, and when I reached the age of eleven the schoolmaster informed me that it was impossible, owing to lack of facilities in that school, to advance me any further. Therefore I was immediately appointed a monitor, and it then became my duty to take charge occasionally of very large classes. I am in a position to know, therefore, how utterly impossible it is, even with the necessary qualifications, to impart any knowledge to the number of people congregated in these classes. In my case, having charge of eighty or ninety children, I found I was simply compelled to devote the whole of my time to maintaining order.

Religion does not seem to have played a major role in Roberts' life: it is never mentioned in his speeches, and he was always in favour of a secular education. However, he sang in the choir at Christ Church, Eaton, while he was at school and used to go out singing on Christmas Eve.[6]

As was normal at that time, his years of education were short by later standards: he left school on 6 April 1882, at the age of thirteen: apparently, he had hopes of becoming a teacher but his ill-health prevented it. A bright boy like Roberts might hope to become an apprentice, but for this money was needed for the premium. In his *Lloyd's Sunday News* article he painted a vivid picture of his father 'working night and day in his little one-roomed cobbler's shop in order that he might save ten pounds for my premium.' However Roberts was fortunate; he won an apprenticeship premium in the printing industry (he does not give any details as to how he did this). Most people have heard of the Norwich printing firm of Jarrold's, but there were also many smaller firms engaged in printing within the city. Roberts was fortunate enough to be given an opportunity in one of these, becoming an apprentice at J. C. Pentney, a printing firm in St Benedict's. He later recalled that his first wage was just 1s. 6d. a week and that the 'printing done by the firm consisted mainly of printing chemist's labels'. While an apprentice he attended evening classes at higher grade and technical schools.

During his apprenticeship, Roberts took up music, learning how to play wind instruments. Again according to his own account, he became so proficient that he was offered a musical career: 'My father, however, was very apprehensive of the temptations to which, he believed, musicians were subjected, and advised me to continue at the printing case.' So, after completing his apprenticeship, he worked as a printer in London between 1889 and 1892. In the latter year, he returned to Norwich, becoming foreman of the printing works at Coleman and Co, the soft drinks manufacturers (not to be confused with Colman's the Norwich mustard business). Roberts soon became a leading trade union man in the city. He was a member of the printers' union, which was called the Typographical Association. He said later that he had founded the Norwich branch, and certainly he soon became its President and secretary. In 1898 he was elected President of the Norwich Trades Council.

This appears to have been in something of a decline during this period. Steven Cherry notes that it was dominated by Liberals, and also that the number of trade unionists affiliated fell from 2,667 in 1899 to 1,200 in 1903. Its campaigns do not seem to have been particularly effective. One was to attempt to persuade the City Council to refrain from paying its road menders less than the standard rate. In 1901, it was involved in a dispute about the dismissal by engineering firm Boulton and Paul of workers because they belonged to a union. The Trades Council offered to act as mediator but the firm declined. In the same year, three men were dismissed by the local Tramways Company, again because they belonged to a union. The Trades Council failed to persuade the Company to give the men their jobs back, but it was able to offer them practical help. It held a public meeting and started a fund, out of which it was able to pay the men ten shillings a week each, with an extra one shilling for each child in the family. Initially this was for eight weeks, but it was extended until such time as they found new jobs.[7]

Roberts had begun his political career as a radical Liberal, and belonged to the local Gladstone Club in Norwich. He joined the Norwich branch of the Independent Labour Party in 1896, two years after its foundation: three years later he was its President. On 4 November 1895, he married Annie, daughter of Horace Marshall, at the Octagon Chapel in Norwich. Horace was a boot and shoe maker working at Bull Close in Norwich in 1891, with a family home on Beaconsfield Road by the time of the marriage. Annie was his eldest child: five years younger than her husband. She had worked before marriage as a dressmaker. No correspondence or personal papers survive, but the marriage appears to have been happy, and lasted throughout Roberts' life: the twenty-fifth anniversary of his marriage was noted in *The Times* in 1920. Their first child was a daughter, Violet Annie, born in 1898. They had three further children, all sons — George Herbert (born 1902), Sidney Henry (born 1907) and Jack Albert (born 1916). By the standards of the time the family was extremely fortunate — all four children grew into adulthood, and all were to outlive their father.

In addition to his union and political work, Roberts was also a member of the Ancient Order of Foresters: his employer J. C. Pentney was an official in the Foresters and may well have introduced Roberts into the Order. It was the largest of the friendly societies operating in Norwich. A Friendly Society provided an income to its members in time of sickness and also provided for payment for medical attendance. These societies were much more popular than trades unions in the first decade of the twentieth century. In 1910, about 16,000 people in Norwich were members of a Friendly Society, while less than 4,000 people were members of trade union. Roberts' own union had just 170 members in Norwich at this date, only a quarter of the people employed in the printing trade in the city.[8]

The Foresters alone claimed 10,000 members in Norwich, including key figures in the city such as Sir Harry Bullard, Jeremiah James Colman, Samuel Hoare and Charles Gilman. Gilman was mayor of Norwich in 1897, the year in which the Order held its 'High Court Meeting' in the city. Roberts always enjoyed entertaining and he threw himself into the occasion, sitting on the Gala and Excursion, United Demonstration and Concert and Ball Committees. All this must have given him contacts outside those he met in his trade union world.[9]

George Roberts had a distinctive character to him — a short man, with a vigorous and alert manner. His photographs give an impression of a vain man, a view clearly shared by the Norwich radical writer Edward Burgess as early as 1905. He described

Roberts being given a photograph of himself by the local I.L.P.: 'in our mind's eye, as it were, we see Mr Roberts, the would-be representative of Norwich, gathered to his own fireside and gazing with fervent admiration at his own photograph'.[10]

Roberts could laugh at himself, on one occasion telling how he had overheard a man in a hotel saying of him, 'they tell me this fellow is smart, talks like a blooming book' — but, typically, went on to say how his oratory had then convinced the man of the righteousness of the Socialist cause! This was the man who led the people of Norwich into the brave new world of Labour Party politics, and who — in the eyes of many — was to betray them.

## Norwich at the end of the nineteenth century

The population of Norwich in 1891 was 100,964, an increase of 13,000 since 1881. Most of the city centre parishes were static in population: the explosion in numbers was in the suburbs, especially to the west in Heigham where almost a third of the city's population now lived. Building regulations controlled the quality of new housing. In 1894, the new houses being erected were going up in streets along the Unthank Road — Gloucester Street, Bury Street, Park Lane and Chester Street. Another area of rapid housing growth was to the north of the city where terraced housing was being developed in Spencer Street, Silver Road and Beaconsfield Road. However these new houses were mainly for the lower middle class. The poorest people still lived in the city centre parishes, in crowded tenements known as *yards*, which had developed behind larger properties facing the street. There would be one entry and shared toilet and water facilities, often of an extremely basic variety. In low-lying areas the yards would be almost permanently wet: these were known as *holes*.

The city's wealth had been built on weaving and the cloth trade but this had declined drastically in the nineteenth century: the number of looms in the city fell from over 5,000 in 1840 to under 1,000 by 1868. The city's decline was halted by a boom in many other activities. The largest single trade became boot and shoe making: firms such as Howlett and White, Haldinstein, Sextons and James Southall employed over 7,500 people in the 1890s. The city's new strength was that it was no longer dependent on one particular trade: other major employers included food and drink makers (including over 2,500 people at Colman's at Carrow), tailoring and dressmaking, and — a Norwich speciality — printing. Norwich also functioned as a marketing, banking and commercial centre to a very large area of the countryside, and had done so since its earliest origins. There was no town of remotely similar size in Norfolk or north Suffolk. Other trades were common to all major towns, such as building and transport: the railway alone employed 900 Norwich men in the 1890s.

To think about what life was like for the disadvantaged in the city in Victorian Norwich is to realise what great steps forward in social history the twentieth century was to see. There was no old age pension, no unemployment or sick pay, no free health service, no universal free education. If you became unable to work for whatever reason, whether through old age, illness or simple failure to find a job, your only recourse was to the Board of Guardians. They might force you into the city Workhouse on Bowthorpe Road, or might pay you a pittance for you to live in your own house: often they would pay in goods such as flour rather than hand over money. There was a continual fear among the Guardians that men who could work might be shirking, preferring to take money from the ratepayers rather than work. For this reason adult males would never be given out-relief: they would have either to go into the Workhouse or work in the city's wood-yard. Women left alone with children, whether widows, abandoned families or single mothers, also had nowhere to turn apart from the Board of Guardians.

The end of the nineteenth century did see the beginnings of an elementary school system. Many schools had been founded by religious groups, whether Church of England, Roman Catholic or Nonconformist. The Education Act of 1870 saw an attempt to fill up the gaps in the system: School Boards were founded to establish elementary schools where the religious bodies had not already done so. The Norwich School Board was established in 1871 and founded almost 20 new schools in the city in its first twenty years. However, working people sending their children to these schools suffered twice over in terms of the family income. Not only did the family lose the few shillings that the child might earn, they also had to pay to send each child, usually one penny or two pence a week. These fees were finally abolished in 1891.

Religion was still a very important part of life in Norwich, as in other towns and cities. There were 35 Anglican churches and almost as many Nonconformist chapels. The population was split roughly 50-50 between 'church' and 'chapel'. There was a small but powerful Roman Catholic community — the Duke of Norfolk was building for them the enormous church on Earlham Road that is now the Roman Catholic cathedral. There was also a strong community of Quakers within the city.

## The political scene

In their comic opera *Iolanthe* in 1882, Gilbert and Sullivan had the chorus:

*That every boy and every gal*
*That's born into the world alive*
*Is either a little Liberal*
*Or a little Conservative*

Ten years later this was no longer true. At the general election of 1892, three 'labour' MPs were elected, John Burns, Joseph Havelock Wilson and James Keir Hardie. All were interesting characters, but only one was really to be a labour politician. Burns was born in Lambeth in 1858, the 16th of the 18 children of Alexander Burns, a Scottish engine fitter, and his wife Barbara. He left school at the age of ten, working first as a barge boy, then in a candle-making factory. He was elected as Independent Labour MP for Battersea in 1892. However he soon became known as a 'Progressive', working with the Liberals. In December 1905 he became President of the Local Government Board, the first working-class man to become a Cabinet minister — but in a Liberal government not a Labour one. Havelock Wilson was leader of the seaman's union. His connection with Labour was very brief. He stood as an official Liberal candidate in 1895 and subsequent elections: in 1906 he was actually opposed by a Socialist, George Lansbury, whose name will recur throughout this book.

The third man elected in 1892 was Keir Hardie: he alone remained loyal to the cause, and was to be the key man in the founding of the Labour party.[11] Keir Hardie was born in Lanarkshire in 1856, the illegitimate son of Mary Keir, a servant: she later married David Hardie, a ships' carpenter. At the age of eight he became a baker's delivery boy. He worked for 12½ hours a day, earning 3s. 6d. a week. One day he came to work late because he had been caring for his brother who was dying: he was sacked and fined a week's wages. At the age of 11 he started work as a coal miner. These were the humble beginnings of the man who was to be the first leader of the Labour Party.

The Party grew out of three different groups dedicated to the Socialist cause. The first was the *Social Democratic Federation*, the S.D.F.. This was founded in 1881, with the object of promoting participation in democratic elections. It was led nationally by Henry Hyndman. The Norwich branch was founded in 1894. One of its local leaders was Walter Smith, later to be Roberts' Parliamentary election agent and eventually a Norwich Labour MP. Smith was born in Thorpe Hamlet in 1872, the son of a labourer and one of a family of ten. He became a shoemaker after an apprenticeship at Sexton's, and became a leading member of the Norwich branch of the Boot and Shoe Operatives' Union. Another local S.D.F. man was Fred Easton, who ran a bookshop in Pitt Street, and was also secretary of the Norwich Peace Association. Born in 1873, he had been a printer at Jarrold's but had to give this up due to poor sight. He advertised his shop with the verse

*Friends of Peace, do you need Reading*
*Of a democratic style,*
*Just try* **Easton's, Pitt Street, Norwich,**
*'Twill be really worth your while.*[12]

By 1908 both Smith and Easton, together with many other S.D.F. supporters, had moved to the Independent Labour Party.

The second group was the *Fabian Society*, founded in 1884. It consisted mainly of intellectuals like Sidney and Beatrice Webb, H. G. Wells and George Bernard Shaw. Their aim was not to establish an independent political party, but to spread their influence within the Liberal Party.

The third group was the *Independent Labour Party* (I.L.P.) founded by Keir Hardie in 1893 with the single aim of getting members of the working class into Parliament. Unlike the other two groups, the Independent Labour Party was committed to winning the support of trade unions to the cause. The Norwich branch was founded in 1894: two of its founding members were Alf Sutton and Herbert Witard, both of whom will appear again in this book. Its first meeting was at the Victoria Hall, during the 1894 Trades Union Congress (T.U.C.) which was held in Norwich that year: this meant that figures of national importance were present, including Keir Hardie himself. Another future Labour leader J. R. Clynes, remembered the Norwich Congress as the time when the union movement committed itself to full-scale nationalisation. A delegate proposed the nationalisation of land and mines: Keir Hardie was on his feet instantly. ' wish to suggest an amendment,' he began in his arresting manner. 'There can be no argument in favour of nationalising lands and mines which does not apply equally to every form of production. If the mines from which we dig minerals are to be nationalised, why not the railways which carry those minerals? Why not the depots where they are deposited, and the works in which they are manufactured. Why shall the landlord be attacked and the capitalist go free?' After much debate his amendment that all means of production, distribution and exchange should be nationalised was carried by 219 votes to 61.[13]

As was customary, the T.U.C. held an open-air rally: in 1894 this was on Mousehold Heath. Keir Hardie and Burns, the chairman of the Congress, were among the speakers: 'unfortunately at the beginning of the procession heavy rain fell, but this did not deter an enormous concourse of people from the city and the neighbouring towns from coming together'. After the Congress was finished Hardie and some friends went for a walk in the Cathedral Close. They stood under 'an old Norman arch' to watch the sun set. In the silence, as the lights in the city were being lit, Hardie began to sing the 23rd psalm and all those present joined in.[14]

However, there was to be no swift success for the new groups. At the 1895 general election, 28 candidates stood for the I.L.P. and four for the S.D.F.: all were defeated, including Keir Hardie himself.

The next step forward came in 1900. Delegates from the I.L.P., the S.D.F. and the Fabian Society met together with delegates representing over half a million trades unionists. They set up the *Labour Representation Committee* (L.R.C.), with James Ramsay MacDonald of the I.L.P. as its secretary. MacDonald was born, an 'illegitimate' child, in Lossiemouth in 1866. He eventually became the first Labour Prime Minister, and — like Roberts himself — was ultimately to be regarded as a traitor to the Labour cause.

The unions agreed to raise a levy from their members to pay the wages of anyone elected as a Member of Parliament under the Committee. It was decided that the candidates did not have to be working men, and that no member of the group would oppose any candidate approved by the L.R.C.

In the 1900 general election two L.R.C. candidates were elected. They were Keir Hardie, re-elected after being defeated in the 1895 election, and Richard Bell. Bell was really a Liberal but the trade union to which he belonged insisted that he fight under the L.R.C. banner. In 1903 they were joined by Arthur Henderson, who won a by-election at Barnard Castle. Henderson was a Scot, born in Glasgow in 1863, and had served his apprenticeship as a moulder in Newcastle. His was an important victory as it was the first time that Labour had won a seat in Parliament when both the Conservatives and the Liberals also put up candidates. The three party system was just beginning to emerge.

It was not just Parliament that Labour wanted to conquer. They also began to put candidates forward at local elections. It must be remembered that not all people yet had the right to vote. There were different rules for different types of election. Men over the age of 21 could vote for Members of Parliament as occupiers, provided they paid rent of at least £10 a year, as householders, or as lodgers, the latter again only if they paid rent above a certain fixed level — five shillings a week for furnished rooms. Occupiers and householders had to be at the same address for a year, lodgers for four months. Women could not vote at all in Parliamentary elections, but some could vote in local elections.

In some ways the late nineteenth century was a more democratic world than that of a century later. Not only did people vote in local government and parliamentary elections, they also had the opportunity to vote for Boards of Guardians of the Poor and, between 1870 and 1902, for School Boards. Left wing groups began to establish themselves on these bodies before they stood in campaigns for Parliament. One reason they could do this was that the franchise was rather wider for these elections than for Parliamentary elections. People who occupied property for which they paid less than £10 a year rent could not vote in Parliamentary elections but they could vote in local elections, both for the council and for the School Board and Board of Guardians.

The most important body at a local level was Norwich City Council. The number of wards in the city had been expanded from eight to 16 in 1892. Each ward had three councillors, one being elected every year and holding his seat for three years. People cared about their council in the early years of the last century. Writing in 1910, Hawkins complained that 'only' 70% of the electorate voted in local elections: a century later the figure is more like 40%![15]

The first I.L.P. man to stand for the City Council was Frederick Hoult, who stood for Heigham ward in 1894. Hoult was a Nottingham man who moved to Norwich in about 1891 to work as a boilermaker at Thorpe station, a job he was to hold all his life. The I.L.P. met at Gordon Hall in Duke Street to put Hoult forward as their candidate, and to announce his policies. The meeting shows how a candidate like Hoult had to produce a programme acceptable to both the S.D.F. and the I.L.P.. Hoult put forward a genuinely radical programme. He wanted the Corporation to hire direct labour rather than contract out, demanded that gas and water be brought under Municipal control, and wanted museums and libraries to open on Sundays. He struck a true Socialist note, demanding 'the abolition of flunkeyism, whether in connection with the Royal wedding, or Royal visits; and the collective ownership of the means of production, distribution and exchange'.

The meeting then considered ideas put forward by the S.D.F.:

1. That wages of Corporation employees should be fixed at 25 shillings a week. The meeting decided that this was not a practical demand.
2. That land be acquired for erecting houses that could be rented by the working class. This was agreed.
3. That municipal washhouses be set up. This provoked much debate, many people saying that women would prefer to wash their clothes in their own home: the proposal was not taken up.
4. That there should be a declaration in favour of municipal control of the liquor trade, buses and other monopolies. Hoult said that this was already in his manifesto and the proposal was 'adopted with enthusiasm'.

Hoult then closed the meeting with a warning: 'there were too many people who believed in making an absurd number of practical promises. He did not believe in so much building castles in the air'.[16]

Hoult's only opponent was George Chamberlin, a former mayor of the city but now in the process of moving from Liberal to Conservative. It was not clear exactly what he was standing as: the Liberal *Eastern Daily Press* thought he was standing as an Independent Unionist. *Daylight*, the local radical newspaper, commented: 'the Liberals make no secret of the fact that they have the choice of two evils and they regard Mr Chamberlin as the least of the two evils'. The ward Liberal association took a line of strict neutrality between the two candidates.[17]

The election was held on 1 November and on the following day the E.D.P. announced a victory for Chamberlin by just 28 votes. This gave the Conservative Walter Whellum an opportunity to condemn the paper. They were all wrong about Chamberlin, he had stood as a Liberal Unionist, and now they had got the voting figures wrong too! In fact Chamberlin polled 390 votes and Hoult 262, a majority of 128.

Nevertheless these 262 people were the first in Norwich to vote Labour: the party was on its way. Despite his radical programme, however, Hoult was not the man to lead them. He very soon became associated with the Liberals rather than with Labour. Hoult died in 1931. His obituary in the E.D.P. describes him as an active member of the Norwich Liberal Association and makes no mention of his being the first person in any Norwich election to stand for the Labour Party! The man to lead Labour to success in Norwich was not Hoult, it was George Roberts.

## The I.L.P. and the School Board

In the year that Roberts joined the I.L.P., that body was turning its attention to another democratic organ, the School Board. The Board was elected *en bloc* every three years. The unusual thing about elections for school boards was the way votes were cast: each voter had as many votes as there were seats on the board, in this case fifteen. However, you could use your votes in any way you wanted – even voting fifteen times for the same candidate if you chose! This was designed as a protection for minority groups. For example, the Roman Catholic community in Norwich was too small to hope to get representation on a School Board elected on a 'one person one vote' system. However, under this system each Catholic voter could put all their votes on one candidate and thus get one representative on the Board. The I.L.P. realised that they could do this too.

In 1896 there were 23 candidates for the 15 seats on the School Board. Alf Sutton of Edinburgh Road stood for the I.L.P., proclaiming, 'I stand primarily for the working class'. He put forward a 15-point programme including free primary, secondary and university education; no class to have more than 40 children; no religious instruction in any Board school; and free meals 'of a substantial and wholesome nature' for needy children. Nor was culture neglected:

> I am in favour of every School having a Piano: the love of Music and
> Art in our Children means a nobler race of Parents in the future.[18]

The I.L.P. joked that they were 'sutton' of getting their man onto the School Board. *Daylight* thought he had a good chance: 'although the I.L.P. is not numerically a strong body it is astonishing what a few resolute men can do'.[19]

In the event Sutton just failed, coming 17th with 6,913 votes: the least successful of the elected candidates had 8,126 votes. One person who was elected was Edward Burgess, the publisher and editor of the independent newspaper *Daylight*. He also issued a *Daylight Annual* satirising Norwich politics. In this he portrayed Sutton as saying that the I.L.P. had sounded the death-knell of Liberal supremacy. He was to prove right, but the process would take far longer than he can have anticipated.[20]

Three years later it was the turn of George Roberts to stand for the School Board for the I.L.P.. Once more his was a deliberately radical programme, which attracted the support of both the I.L.P. and the S.D.F.. He campaigned for the raising of the school leaving age to sixteen, free maintenance for all school children, and for class sizes to be restricted to a maximum of 30 — and also for a purely secular education. This time there were 19 candidates for the 15 seats. Roberts came sixth with 11,387 votes. This was the first victory for Labour in Norwich at any level.

Once again, *Daylight* appreciated the significance of Roberts' success:

> Mr Roberts makes no pretensions whatever to look after the ratepayers' pockets. A more pronounced or outspoken address than that of the I.L.P. candidate could not be conceived. No one was left in any doubt as to what Mr Roberts would do if he had the power. His success at the poll is all the more striking. To secure 11,387 votes on a strict Socialist programme is an accomplishment which the local Socialists may well be proud of, and I congratulate the thoroughness they have manifested. The members of the I.L.P. and the S.D.F. have worked like Trojans and they have their reward.

As the only I.L.P. candidate, Roberts would have known that in practice any radical measures he put forward would be massively out-voted. He could be as radical as he liked, and blame the rest of the Board if his policies were not put into practice. The plan was a successful one, and he was successful again three years later. It was in this year (1902) that Edward Burgess described Roberts as 'an ambitious windbag': Burgess was a Liberal and so a bitter rival! In any case, Roberts' role came to an end very soon after the election: the School Boards were abolished under the Education Act of 1902. Their functions were taken over by the city council. This experiment in local democracy was at an end.

Roberts enjoyed his time on the Board. A few years later he was to recall: 'my School Board work was most congenial to me, for I am convinced that until we have an educated, intelligent democracy, it is hopeless to look for permanently improved conditions of life among the working classes'.[21]

Roberts' School Board career also gave him a new interest, and one that was to last for the rest of his life. This interest was in the care and education of the blind. The Blind and Deaf Act of 1893 had ordered local authorities to provide 'efficient' education for these groups. The only provision for the education of the blind in East Anglia was the Institute for the Blind in Norwich, but this was intended to supply training in skills like basket making, rather than elementary education. Roberts was present at a conference held in the Guildhall in March 1901 which debated the best way forward. No decision was made at the time, but seeds were sown which led to the establishment of the East Anglian School for the Deaf and Blind at Gorleston in 1912.

## The Board of Guardians

Elected Poor Law Guardians were set up for groups or unions of parishes under the New Poor Law Act of 1834. However, Norwich itself was different: it had set up Guardians to regulate the poor of all the city parishes, including the suburbs (but not the Cathedral Close, which stood aloof), as early as 1712. The system was reformed under local Acts of 1831 and 1863. After 1863 the Norwich Board was organised just like any of the other Boards. The Board of Guardians had 48 members. They were elected *en bloc* every three years. Three people were elected for each district, unlike the School Board, which was elected for the whole city. Three I.L.P. candidates stood in the 1895 election, but without success. The first 'labour' man elected to the Board of Guardians was Walter Smith of the S.D.F.. He polled 321 votes on his first attempt in 1901, and was elected three years later. One other radical candidate was elected in the following year, Rev W. R. Cummings a nominee of the I.L.P., but he left the city soon after. The I.L.P. nominated Billy Holmes as their candidate to replace Cummings on the Board of Guardians. He was a strong candidate, a local man born in Norwich in 1873, and working at Colman's mustard factory in Carrow. He was the I.L.P.'s organising secretary and had fought unsuccessfully in the previous Guardians' election. He was defeated once more, but by only 63 votes.

Smith, like Roberts on the School Board, had to spend three years as the single Socialist on an elected Board, but other Labour men eventually followed. Other pre-war Labour people on the Board included Fred Jex and Billy Hinds.[22]

## Success on the City Council

The City Council soon had 'labour' members too. Herbert Witard stood for Coslany Ward as a Socialist in 1901. Witard was something of a character, having run away to sea at the age of 13. A quarter of a century later he recalled:

> When I was 10, I was selling newspapers at the corner of London Street — badly clothed, often almost bootless, labouring under exceptional difficulties. I was at work after school hours at eleven when I handed my newspaper business over to my next brother. At 13 I was a cabin boy on a fishing smack, and had, at least, this advantage that we were not allowed to wash (Laughter) ... I am not exaggerating when I say that at the age of 16 it would have been an almost impossible task for me to have written a letter.[23]

Witard was unsuccessful. He tried again in 1902, once more without success. In the same year as Witard's second defeat, the political writer Fred Henderson *was* elected to the council. He could be described as the first Socialist on the council — and does so describe himself on a hand-written note on his copy of his election manifesto held at the Norfolk Record Office.[24] However he did not stand for the Labour Party, but ran independently as a Progressive candidate. Nevertheless, in practical terms, he was a genuine Radical. He had been a leader of the 'Ham Run Riot' of January 1887. Over 500 unemployed men had gathered in Norwich Market Place. Henderson and Charles Mowbray tried to obtain relief for them from the mayor: when the mayor refused and called the men 'loafers', Henderson and Mowbray told them 'that the matter was in their own hands'. The men then went on a looting spree of food shops: Henderson and Mowbray were sentenced to prison for their part in the rioting. They became the last men to be forced to work on the treadmill in Norwich Castle Gaol.

Witard tried yet again the following year, once more for the Coslany ward and this time specifically for the I.L.P.. His 1903 campaign literature was unashamedly directed at the working class voter:

> WORKERS! Vote for Yourselves by VOTING FOR WITARD
> The Landlord wants big Rents for little Houses...
> The Employer wants long Hours for short Wages...
> The Worker wants big Healthy Houses for low rents and Higher Wages for Shorter Hours.

It was third time lucky. Although opposed by both a Liberal and a Conservative, Witard won a decisive victory. He wasted no time in making his mark on council business. Just four weeks after his election, he put forward a motion demanding that the council set up a Labour Bureau to co-ordinate the various work programmes it was undertaking and make sure the unemployed were aware of them.

## Parliament

Local elections were just the start, of course, the final step was Parliament. In Parliamentary terms, Norwich was an unusual type of seat – it was a *two-member constituency*. Every elector had two votes and two MPs were elected. Naturally where two candidates of the same party stood, people tended to vote for them both, but in many elections parties were not able to field two candidates. Electors then had difficult choices to make as to how to cast their second vote. This was to be a key factor in every Parliamentary election discussed in this book. The last general election had been held in 1892. The two men elected MPs for Norwich were Samuel Hoare, a Conservative, and Jeremiah James Colman, a Liberal and supporter of the Prime Minister William Gladstone. Both were men of great local importance and had been the city's MPs since 1886. The Hoare family lived at Cromer and were bankers by profession. Colman was the head of Colman's, the mustard and food manufacturers in the city. He lived at Carrow Abbey and the family were known for their generosity to their employees, supplying housing, schools and nursing care.

There was a general election in 1895. Colman decided not to stand again: he was 65 years old and his wife was very ill. The Conservatives fielded two strong candidates, Hoare and Sir Harry Bullard, the Norwich brewer. The Liberals also put up two candidates but the Labour Party was not yet ready to stand. In the event, the Conservatives won both seats. However, in the next general election held in 1900 there were no choices at all for the *Norwich Electorate*. The two Conservatives – Hoare and Bullard – were elected unopposed. The I.L.P. did suggest to Roberts that he stand, but he declined to do so. The election was held during the Boer War and the mood of the country was extremely jingoistic. Roberts was probably shrewd enough to realise that any Labour candidate would have no chance of success. The Liberal Party no doubt took the same view.

Financing campaigns was a problem for Labour candidates, as few of their supporters were wealthy. The greater part of their funds came from the trade unions. Few records survive of local branches, but the records of the Norwich Electrical Trades Union show that they were raising money for a labour candidate from 1901 onwards.[25]

Labour and the Liberals were working together as allies rather than as opposing parties. In 1903 Herbert Gladstone, the Liberal Chief Whip, and Ramsay MacDonald came to an agreement that was to be crucial to the future of the Labour Party. In the past there had been a few cases where Liberal and 'Labour' candidates had agreed not to oppose each other, which had resulted in a tiny number of 'Lib-Lab' Members of Parliament: one, Henry Broadhurst, had even become a junior minister, the first representative of Labour to hold government office. Gladstone and MacDonald now put this local co-operation on a more formal basis and on a much larger scale. They agreed that Labour would be given a free run in forty to fifty seats at the next general election, in return for giving support to Liberal candidates elsewhere. Norwich was one of these seats — Labour and the Liberals would each put up just one candidate so that radically minded electors could vote for both.

However, things were not to work out so smoothly. Sir Harry Bullard died at the end of 1903. Hoare, of course, continued as an MP, so this meant a by-election at which the voters of Norwich had just one vote each: just one candidate would be elected. Both the Liberals and Labour put up candidates in the by-election. Many people on the national Labour Representation Committee thought this broke the spirit of the agreement with the Liberals. They included Will Crooks and Richard Bell. One of the keenest workers in Tillett's cause was Fred Henderson, who gave speeches to working men urging them to vote for Tillett rather than Roberts. He even said that anyone who voted for Roberts was in effect voting for the Conservative candidate, Ernest Wild. Roberts would only split the anti-Conservative vote.

Four Labour leaders, Keir Hardie, Ramsay MacDonald, John Hodge and Arthur Henderson came to Norwich to help in the campaign. In their hotel, they discussed Roberts' prospects. The first three all thought he would win by varying majorities. Hodge turned to Henderson to ask his opinion. 'He was pressed, and finally said: 'I think you are all wrong; there won't be any majority. The Liberal will come in first, the Tory second, and Roberts will be a bad third'.[26]

## By-Election January 1904:

| L J TILLETT (Liberal) | 8,576 |
| E E Wild (Conservative) | 6,756 |
| G H Roberts (I.L.P.) | 2,440 |

*Daylight Annual* had a satirical verse appropriate for the occasion, with a sting in its tail:

*'Twas a frosty winter morning, just the day I like t'enjoy,*
*When I waked and looked out early, puzzled how my time t'employ.*
*Just then I heard a 'rat-tat-tat', and paused a tick or two,*
*Then I went down to the front door - as I'd nothing else to do.*
*'If you please, are you George Roberts?' asked a voice I knew quite well.*
*I replied 'Of course I am, lad', as into my arms he fell.*

# 'WHAT MR ROBERTS WOULD DO IF HE HAD THE POWER'

*Said he 'There's an election on, and the I.L.P. want you'.*
*My word, I fairly jumped for joy — for I'd nothing else to do.*

*The fight was fought, — and lost, of course — but I played my little game,*
*And if you say 'Oh Roberts, fie!' — you will see I'm not to blame,*
*For when it was all over, they said 'Here's a post for you!'*

(Spoken: *Yes, my lads, a post worth a cool two hundred and fifty pounds per annum, with plenty of travelling, heaps of meetings and all that sort of thing. Of course, I hesitated about throwing up a situation worth less than half that amount, but ---*)

*Sung: Did I take it? Well, yes, rather! - For I'd nothing else to do.*[27]

The 'job' was to be the southern organiser of the Typographical Association. One of his first acts was to speak at the 1904 T.U.C. in favour of free school meals:

> He hardly thought the word 'free' the proper one, because by improving their physique they would become more profitable members of the state. To be well-fed should be regarded as the right of every school child in the Empire.[28]

Despite his by-election setback, Roberts was on his way up the political ladder.

# 'Some working inordinately long hours while others are denied work': Labour in Norwich 1904-1914

## The national scene

In December 1905 the Conservative government led by Arthur Balfour collapsed The Liberal leader, Henry Campbell Bannerman formed a minority government. His cabinet included two ministers who were achieving this rank for the first time, John Burns and David Lloyd George. A general election followed at the beginning of 1906. The Liberals won 377 seats, a majority of 84 over all the other parties combined. The Conservatives won just 137 seats, and even these were divided between Conservative Unionists and Liberal Unionists. No less than 53 'Labour' MPs were elected. Of these 29 were L.R.C. men: the others were mainly officials of the miners' union, which was not yet affiliated to the L.R.C. The miners became part of the Labour Party in 1909.

In 1908-9 the Osborne Judgement decreed that unions could not raise a compulsory levy from their members to pay the salaries of MPs. Some 16 Labour MPs found their salaries cut off. The situation was resolved in 1911 when it was agreed that MPs should be paid by the State: their salary was to be £400 a year.

By then, however, two further general elections had been fought, both in 1910 and both over the issue of the power of the House of Lords. In 1909 the Liberal Chancellor of the Exchequer Lloyd George, supported by the Labour Party, had put forward a radical budget. This including imposing duties on profits made by landowners as their property rose in value. The House of Lords, many of whom derived their income from their land, would not pass the budget. Asquith at once called an election which was held in January 1910. The result saw the two major parties neck and neck. The Liberals won 275 seats, the Conservatives just two fewer. Labour lost a dozen seats, falling back to 40. There were also 82 Irish Nationalist MPs. Some Labour MPs wanted to distance themselves from the Liberals to show they were an independent party. However, they did not want to bring in a Conservative government. In any case, both the Labour Party and the

Irish Nationalists supported the Liberals on the big issue of the day, the need to curb the power of the House of Lords.

Asquith wanted to create a large number of Liberal peers to swamp the Conservative majority in the Lords. The king, Edward VII, said he could only do this after a second general election. Edward died in May 1910, but his successor, George V, took the same line. Asquith called another general election, which was held in December. The result was almost exactly the same as in January. Liberals and Unionists each had 272 seats but the Liberals could rely on the support of the 42 Labour MPs and the 84 Irish Nationalists. The House of Commons passed an Act restricting the powers of the Lords in rejecting bills that the Commons passed. The House of Lords had no choice but to give way and accept the new legislation.

## Events in Norwich

Labour were beginning to make their mark on the City Council. In 1905 Witard put forward a motion that the council should petition the Prime Minister in favour of the School Meals Bill then before Parliament. Many Liberals and Conservatives walked out of the chamber immediately before his motion was raised at the meeting of the council on 15 July. As there was no quorum the session was terminated. He repeated this demand at the September meeting of the council. This time George White amended the wording of the motion to stress the concern of the Council about 'the question of underfed schoolchildren in Elementary Schools' and urging the Prime Minister to deal with the issue at the earliest possible moment in the next session of Parliament. This motion was carried.[29]

A second I.L.P. man, Billy Holmes, was elected for Coslany in 1905, followed by Arthur Dunnett for Fye Bridge ward in 1906. Dunnett was a genuine local candidate having been born in the ward: he had left school at the age of eleven and worked in a garret as a bootmaker. Walter Smith, standing under the title of Socialist, was successful for Mousehold in the same year. Although the I.L.P. and the S.D.F. were separate groups, they were working together in a common cause. They never put up candidates against each other. The I.L.P. newspaper, the *Norwich Elector*, recognised Smith's qualities: 'Walter Smith is a telling and effective speaker, and his clear, clean, incisive arguments, and his powerful pleading, have won innumerable converts to Socialism'.[30]

The Labour Party in Norwich was gearing up for the next general election as well as expanding its membership on the City Council. As mentioned above, it had started a monthly newspaper in 1905, the *Norwich Elector*. At first this was wary of Roberts, saying: 'the first thing to make quite clear is that Mr George

Roberts who is now before the electors as a Labour candidate is NOT THE CANDIDATE OF THE I.L.P.'. The paper pointed out that Roberts was being put forward by a trades union (the Typographical Association) and was afraid that Roberts would put his union interests before those of the I.L.P.. However it decided to support him, and leave it to post-election discussion to decide if he would be accepted as an official I.L.P. man.[31]

The Party held a May Day rally in Norwich Market Place on 7 May 1905 – Roberts, Smith, Witard and Holmes were all there. The Electrical Trades Union thought of the rally as part of Roberts' election campaign, bringing out their union banner for the occasion, and their minutes refer to Roberts as 'our worthy Labour Parliamentary candidate'.

Later in the month, Smith was appointed election agent and committee rooms were opened at 17 White Lion Street. Roberts held five public meetings in Norwich in August, which the Norwich Elector, naturally, thought were 'in every way a great success'. He was able to intervene successfully in a labour dispute at Southall's, a Norwich shoemaking firm. Significantly for his future career, he was in demand throughout Britain as a speaker, supporting Socialist candidates as far away as Plymouth, Cardiff and Glasgow. Roberts was becoming known throughout the Labour movement for his oratory.

In December 1905 it was announced that the general election would be held in January. As the Norwich Elector put it: 'The fight has begun! The respective candidates are preparing for the fray'. Roberts had the support of the Labour Representation Committee, who urged that past differences be forgotten and every effort be made to elect him. The Norwich Elector published messages of support for Roberts from 36 other Labour candidates, including Keir Hardie and Ramsay MacDonald, Keir Hardie writing: 'Working men in Norwich are fortunate in having one of the straightest, clearest and most conscientious men in the Labour movement as their candidate.'[32]

The local Liberal newspaper, the Eastern Daily Press, which, of course, reached a very much wider audience, was supporting Roberts as the recipient of the second votes of Liberal supporters:

> We recommend Liberal electors to read the two excellent speeches
> which Mr Roberts has made this week in Norwich, to note their
> energy and their grasp of principles, and we think that they will
> agree with us that the city ought to congratulate itself upon having
> a working man capable of conducting a candidature.[33]

Roberts' election manifesto included a commitment to adult suffrage for both men and women. He was strongly in favour of Free Trade. As a man with a

School Board background he had views on education issues: 'Teachers should not be subjected to sectarian tests, but be appointed upon merit and qualification for their work… I desire that State provision be made to feed schoolchildren, so that poverty shall be no hindrance to the acquisition of the highest Education by the children of all classes'. As a trade unionist he thought unemployment would be the key issue at the election and he distributed an article he had written on the subject. This recommended introducing a maximum working day of eight hours. This would 'modify the terrible modern paradox of some working inordinately long hours whilst others are denied work'. He also advocated raising the school leaving age, and recommended a system of education to develop 'each child's particular aptitudes'. Once more Labour's big guns were brought in to support him: Keir Hardie himself held a meeting at St. Andrew's Hall on 5 January 1906.

At last, the day of the election came. The count took place at Blackfriars' Hall, and just before midnight the figures were flashed on a screen at the Guildhall. There was a great swing to the Liberals at the election in the country as a whole, and the Labour candidates benefited from this, leading to a triumph for George Roberts:

## General Election 1906:

| G H ROBERTS (I.L.P.) | 11,059 |
| --- | --- |
| L J TILLETT (Liberal) | 10,972 |
| E E Wild (Conservative) | 7,460 |

The Liberal-Labour pact had worked, both in local and national terms. Over 10,000 Norwich voters had cast their votes for both Roberts and Tillett. Nationally Roberts was one of 29 L.R.C. members elected, to be soon joined by another. Almost all had only been elected, however, because the Liberal Party had not put up candidates to oppose them. One of the first acts of the Labour Representation Committee after its election was to change its name to the Labour Party.[34]

Most people still saw the Liberals and Labour as friends and allies. *Daylight Annual*, as usual, had a verse for the occasion. The newspaper imagined Roberts as singing:

*I took my seat in Parliament,*
*With Louis and pals at my side.*
*And all those who elected me to that seat,*
*Looked on me with hope and pride.*
*I had no riches to count or to boast,*

*Or high ancestral name,*
*But that which I had, which charmed me most*
*Your confidence which gave me fame,*
*And added MP to my name — and added MP.*
*MP you'll add again.*[35]

The new Labour MPs included several, apart from Roberts, who feature in this book. One was George Barnes who had made his name fighting for the Old Age Pension. Barnes was born at Loch, Dundee, in 1859: his father was a journeyman machine maker. The family moved to London and, at the age of thirteen, Barnes became a clerk in a jute mill. Others included John Hodge, who was to become a close friend and ally of Roberts. Hodge was born in Muirkirk in Scotland in 1856: his father was a steel-worker. He passed an examination for work as a pupil teacher but was disqualified as it was found that he was still under thirteen.

*The Labour Parliamentary party after the 1906 election. Roberts is in the centre of the front row.*

After his election, Roberts gave an interview to *Pearson's Weekly*, describing his background. He said that because of his ill-health he was thrown upon books:

> The works of Charles Dickens in particular had much to do with shaping my view of life, giving me a deep and abiding sympathy with the poor and suffering. Then my health, and especially my weak voice, worried me, and I made up my mind to improve my physical condition, to this end going in for physical exercises, and joining an educational society, where I took up the study of physiology and biology. I became particularly enamoured of Darwin's works, and acquired a grasp of, and enduring belief in, his theory of evolution,

the principles of which, I may say, have been a guiding factor in my life. I suppose one reason why I have got on is that I never associate myself with any party or question except after careful enquiry and reflection. But when convinced of the right and justice of a cause I bestow upon it a constant and steadfast devotion, without regard to any man's power or desire to count any man's favour.[36]

Fifteen years later, looking back, he thought it was his wide reading that had made him so flexible in his thinking: 'The more knowledge we acquire the more obvious become the human limitations. It is only the half-educated who adopt the dogmatic pose.'[37]

## George Roberts in Parliament

The Labour Members of Parliament formed their own party and elected Keir Hardie as their leader. He appointed Roberts and Fred Jowett as his parliamentary secretaries. Hardie very soon came to appreciate Roberts' qualities as an organiser. He sent him a copy of the poems of Robert Burns as a Christmas present in December 1906. His accompanying letter said:

I should have found the duties of my position much more irksome but for your assistance. If circumstances so ordain that I again occupy the position of chairman next session I sh[oul]d like nothing better than to again have your services.[38]

The following year he appointed Roberts as Whip of the Labour MPs in Parliament. In 1912 he became Chief Whip, a position which was his stepping stone to high office.

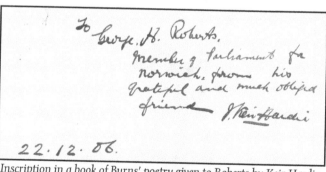

Inscription in a book of Burns' poetry given to Roberts by Keir Hardie.

The Liberal government elected in 1906 was genuinely radical. Some of its measures were specifically fought for by the Labour party. They included a topic dear to Roberts' heart, the provision of free school meals. The School Meals Act of 1906 enabled local authorities to provide free meals to needy schoolchildren. Typically for a Liberal government it did not compel them to do so — however, by 1914 half the local authorities in the country were providing free meals.

Roberts was an active Parliamentarian, especially concerned with employment and trade union questions. In his first speech, on 26 February 1906, he addressed labour issues, asking the Government to move further in the direction of the eight-hour day and saying that his party was 'keenly alive' to the problem of unemployment. He showed his background by speaking in praise of the Liberal Cabinet Minister John Burns. He said working men were proud of Burns as coming from the working classes and of being worthy of a seat in the Cabinet. He also put down many questions to ministers, beginning with two in March 1906. One concerned the number of men laid off in Portsmouth Dockyard, the other was about two men in Bedford who had been sentenced to five years in prison merely for breaking windows.

In December of the same year he acted as a good constituency MP, drawing the attention of the Commons to problems of the unemployed in Norwich. He asked Burns, who was President of the Local Government Board, if he was aware that 962 unemployed people in Norwich were registered with the Distress Committee in the city. Almost 700 of these people qualified for assistance under the Unemployed Workmen's Act. The Committee had applied for a share of the money allocated to local Distress Committees by the Government under the Act. It had not yet received any of the money. Burns replied that he was looking into the situation. Roberts' intervention was successful. The Local Government

THE POLITICAL MARIAGE DE CONVENANCE.
Louis :—" It's no good Roberts. If you want to remain M.P. you must recognise the alliance."

*Roberts of the I.L.P. still tied in partnership with the Liberal Louis Tillett. A 'Daylight' cartoon.*

Board contributed £2,000 to the Norwich Distress Committee under the terms of the Act in the financial year 1906-7.[39]

Roberts was now committed to Socialist values: in a speech in Parliament on 10 April 1907 in a debate about local authorities and land purchase, he explicitly stated that he was in favour of the public ownership of land. In March 1909, he spoke in a debate on the Trade Boards Bill, which proposed Boards to be set up in various trades, on which both employers and employed would be represented: they would fix minimum wages within the trade. Roberts was loyal to his union roots. He said that 'no clause will ever be perfectly satisfactory unless it is based on strict trade union principles'. However, unlike Hardie and some of the other Labour MPs, Roberts was

THE DAILY GRAPHIC, SATURDAY, MAY 4, 1907.

COMPULSORY WEIGHING AND MEASUREMENTS BILL SECOND READING

Mʳ G ROBERTS (PRINTER) MOVER

Mʳ J. HODGE (ENGINEER) (SECONDER)

Mʳ GLADSTONE "THE GOVERNMENT, THEREFORE, ACCEPT THE SECOND READING OF THIS BILL

Mʳ SAMUEL

THE MILDEST OF MILD CRITICISM FROM LORD BALCARRES

SIR W. HOLLAND ON LIMITED PARTNERSHIPS

A SHORT SITTING IN THE HOUSE OF COMMONS.

*The Daily Graphic, May 4, 1907, commenting on a bill moved by Roberts.*

never a republican. He spoke approvingly of what he saw as the people's deep appreciation of the monarchy.[40]

The most revolutionary act of this Parliament was the introduction of Old Age Pensions under an Act passed in 1908. Roberts was naturally a supporter, and, like many other Members of Parliament, concentrated his fire on the limited effect of the proposals: anyone who had been in receipt of poor relief was excluded from receiving a pension. Roberts cited two local examples in his speech. One was a seventy-four year old man who lived in Norwich, 'a sober, industrious an respectable man who had worked all his life'. His wife became ill, so he had t stop working to look after her — and had to accept poor relief while he did s After her death, he returned to work but under the Bill he would be stigmatise as a pauper all his life and never qualify for the new pension.

Roberts then talked about a Norfolk village, where a friend of his was the paris clergyman. The parish had 345 inhabitants, ten of which were over seventy (th seems a very low percentage by the standards of a century later, showing ho low life expectancy was in those days). Of the ten, seven had at some time bee on poor relief, so would never qualify for the pension. Two others would fail th income test — they were receiving small sums of money from other sources. Th tenth was very frail, and would not 'be able to survive the inquisitorial tests of th measure'. Two or three of these people had been forced to get poor relief on because they had been giving a shilling a week out of their wages of about twelv shillings a week to support aged parents. All ten had led industrious lives, yet n a single person in this Norfolk village would get the pension.

In fact, Roberts had raised the issue of the Poor Law and its treatment of th elderly a couple of months earlier, in March 1908. He brought to the attentio of the House the case of Frederick William Brown, an agricultural labourer c Blofield, just east of Norwich. Brown had been sentenced to 21 days in priso for arrears under a maintenance order to help pay toward his elderly father, wh was in the Workhouse. The Blofield Guardians of the Poor thought he shoul contribute to the costs of keeping him there. Roberts pointed out that Brown wa only earning twelve shillings a week, which was the normal farm wage in Norfol at this time. Roberts was answered by John Burns, as President of the Loc Government Board, who had clearly done his homework. He agreed that Brown wage was only twelve shillings, but pointed out that with his extra payments fo summer and harvest work, his average wage over the year was more like fourtee or fifteen shillings a week. What is more, Brown had two brothers, who, like hir were single men with no children, and who were earning the same level of wage The Guardians thought that each of these men should pay one shilling a wee towards the upkeep of their father. Burns did agree that the whole question c contributions by relations was being considered by the Poor Law Commission.

In 1910 there were two general elections. The Liberal-Labour pact still held: i Norwich the Conservatives put up two candidates, the Liberals and Labour on each. Tillett decided not to stand again, but the Liberals put up a strong candidat the barrister and King's Counsel, Sir Frederick Low. The result produced a sma swing to the Conservatives but they were still well behind the Radical candidate

## General Election January 1910:

| SIR FREDERICK LOW, KC (Liberal) | 11,257 |
| --- | --- |
| GEORGE ROBERTS (Labour) | 11,119 |
| Sir Samuel Hoare (Conservative) | 8,480 |
| H G Snowden (Conservative) | 7,981 |

Roberts was back in Parliament. Having spent time on the Norwich School Board, he naturally took an interest in education issues. It was during a debate on classroom sizes in April 1910 that he described his days as a monitor, cited in the first chapter of this book. He had started this speech in typically forthright style:

> When you have the spectacle in our midst of some people being able to spend, say, £1,000 on training a dog for the Waterloo Cup, or thousands of pounds on training a horse for a race, in my opinion the nation is losing sight of the principle of true economy being the wisest expenditure, and I do claim that the nation would be better served if that money, which, in my opinion, is thus squandered, was devoted to providing every child in the nation with the fullest form of education that it could assimilate.

He went on to talk about raising the school-leaving age, something that he had always favoured. There had been a suggestion that the age should be raised in urban areas only, so that young country children could continue to leave to go into farm work, where it was said they were needed. Roberts was scathing, comparing the idea to the old system where very young children worked in factories. The school leaving age should be raised for everyone: 'The agricultural labourers' child is just as capable of assimilating education as children in other classes and can claim just as much right for a share in education facilities as if it had been born in one of our urban areas.'

In May 1910, over one hundred farm labourers in St. Faiths, just north of Norwich, went on strike for an extra shilling a week, and a half-day on Saturdays. With his farming background, Roberts naturally had something to say, speaking out in favour of the strikers. However, after about ten months of struggle, the labourers had to admit defeat, some accepting their former wages while others who had taken action were victimised. Roberts was to be reminded of the strike by hecklers thirteen years later.[41]

He spoke about Norfolk farm labourers in a debate on financial estimates on 14 July 1911:

> In my part of the country, whence I hail, there are agricultural labourers working for 11 shillings, 12 shillings, 13 shillings or 14 shillings a week. I remember once being contradicted in this House because I stated that there were some working for 11 shillings a week. I am prepared to testify to this fact. There are relatives of my own working for rates as low as that. Large sections of these men are afraid to agitate owing to the fact that as soon as they are remarked they are given notice to leave their particular cottages, and there are no other houses available. Therefore they are compelled by sheer stress of economic circumstances to acquiesce in conditions which I feel are truthfully referred to as little removed from actual slavery.

The second election of 1910 had taken place in December. Once again the Liberals and Labour each put up just one candidate. However, this time the Conservatives also fielded only one candidate, William Dyson. Dyson was an ex-miner. He made much of his claim to be a working man who disliked the politicisation of the trade union movement. His campaign advertising put Dyson forward as 'Will Workman — the Working Man's Candidate'. Roberts stressed that the main issue at the election was the House of Lords. He said in the Commons on 15 May 1911 that the Labour Party queried the need for a second chamber at all, but conceded that most people thought one was needed. He thought it should not have power over Parliamentary Bills but should be merely consultative. He took the opportunity of the second election to remind voters of his personal commitment to universal suffrage. (In fact Dyson was also in favour of votes for women, but on the same terms as was currently being given to men, not a universal suffrage.) The result was much the same as that of eleven months before.

## General Election December 1910:

| SIR FREDERICK LOW, KC (Liberal) | 10,149 |
| GEORGE ROBERTS (Labour) | 10,003 |
| W Dyson (Conservative) | 7,758 |

Once more *Daylight Annual* had a verse for the occasion, this time implying that Roberts was prepared to do almost anything to remain a Member of Parliament:

*This Socialist member*
*On the tenth of December*
*Just patted himself as he said:*
*'I'll be yours Mister KC*
*If your men vote for me,*
*We'll be politically wed,*
*For whoever's elected,*
*Amongst the rejected,*
*Yours truly we will never see;*
*I shall still be MP.*[42]

The Liberal/Labour pact was holding. Over 10,000 people voted for both Low and Roberts in January 1910, and over 9,000 in December. Only 209 voters were so committed to Labour that they voted for Roberts alone in January: this figure rose in December, but was still only 562. As it turned out, there was not to be another general election for eight years. By then things were very different.

In fact, in 1910, after just four years in Parliament, Roberts had been seriously considered for a post in Government. During the constitutional crisis arising out of the refusal of the House of Lords to approve Lloyd George's budget, Asquith gave serious consideration to forming an all-party coalition, and authorised Lloyd George to undertake the negotiations. MacDonald was prepared to take up a place in the coalition cabinet, and the Labour Party were offered two Under-Secretaries. MacDonald chose Henderson and Roberts for the positions: however, both rejected the idea. As Francis Williams noted, 'they refused the Lloyd George offer brought to them by Macdonald because they had a much firmer understanding than he of the consequences such an all-party coalition would have upon the organisation of the Labour Party and upon the mind of its rank and file. They were committed to an extent he never was to those trade-union and working-class loyalties which have, even in its most difficult days, always given the Labour party a cohesion that has saved it from disaster'. The scheme collapsed in any case as the Conservatives refused to co-operate, but shows the high position that Roberts had already reached within the Labour Party, equal with Henderson and only behind MacDonald himself.

Roberts continued to be active in the Trades Union Movement. At the 1911 Trades Union Congress he showed his usual independence of thought, disagreeing with some of the proposals put forward. He spoke against their proposals on the Insurance Bill as he thought they would put a burden on the Friendly Societies. He also disliked a proposal which gave trades unions a special role with regard to unemployment pay: 'I have always maintained that State aid for unemployment ought to be based on citizenship and not upon membership of any particular organisation'. As always, his forthright views were not always welcome. One delegate complained that Roberts had spoken no less than six times during the week while other delegates had not had any opportunity to speak at all![40]

Roberts had gone abroad with a Labour group to Germany in 1909. He kept the menu of a dinner in Cologne on 1 June among his personal papers. He got another taste of foreign travel in 1911. He was one of two of the Trades Union Congress delegates present at the American Convention of Labour in Atlanta, Georgia. The habit never deserted him, as we shall see. In 1913 he was in Dublin with Henderson and Barnes as part of a Labour Party delegation in support of the Dublin tramway workers. At a mass meeting held on 7 September, Roberts protested at the actions of the Irish police the previous weekend 'which had led to the death of two of our comrades'.

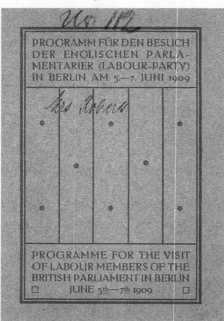

*The programme for Labour MPs' trip to Berlin, 1909.*

In 1914, Roberts and Labour Party colleagues went to Denmark to study agricultural conditions there. The country had been seen as a model ever since Henry Rider Haggard had published *Rural Denmark* in 1911, backing it up with a series of articles in *The Times*. Haggard, like Roberts, a Norfolk man born and bred, is best known for novels like *King Solomon's Mines* and *She*. However, he was also a serious writer on agricultural issues, his *Rural England* (1902) having exposed the terrible conditions of farmers and farm labourers. He had visited Denmark and been impressed. Farmers worked in co-operatives on nationalised land – and exported agricultural products worth £20 million a year. The country was naturally seen as an example to follow by supporters of land nationalisation like George Roberts.[44]

Roberts was one of several members of the small group of Labour MPs to take up the idea of proportional representation. Another supporter, Philip Snowden, reckoned it could give the party a hundred MPs, which it would otherwise take a generation to achieve. Roberts spoke in favour of proportional representation in the Commons on 30 March 1910, saying that in his home town

NORWICH PARLIAMENTARY ELECTION, 1910.

*Roberts' 1910 election leaflet.*

he had seen the Labour Party gaining large numbers of votes but failing to obtain representation because of a combination of other political voices. In his view, 'every party has the right to representation that its numerical strength warrants'. However, he conceded that this was not official Labour Party policy: 'On this question I am in the position of being unable to speak on behalf of the party with whom I customarily act', a position he would find himself in more and more often in his career.

Roberts was now seen as one of the leaders of the small Labour group in Parliament. He was one of five Labour men to speak in favour of an amendment they had put forward to the King's speech in February 1912. The amendment urged a minimum wage, and nationalisation of railways and mines. It was, of course, heavily defeated. The speeches of the five leaders were later printed as a pamphlet and sold for a penny.

The Labour Party at this time had a chairman of its Executive Committee, elected every year by the Committee members. In 1912-3, the choice fell upon Roberts. In this capacity, he became directly involved in the issue of women's suffrage. In 1912,

DOING A LITTLE WASHING.

*Roberts pictured as Labour Party whip [from 'Daylight'.].*

Roberts and other Labour Party leaders, Ramsay MacDonald, Arthur Henderson and Keir Hardie met with the leaders of the National Union of Women's Suffrage Societies. The Labour Party men confirmed that they were committed to women's suffrage. This was the first time that a major political party had made this commitment. However the party still had fewer than 50 MPs so its support was not significant. The *Suffragette* accused the Party of dodging the issue where it could. It claimed that at the annual conference of the Labour Party in 1913 Roberts, as chairman, had been sent a letter requesting that delegates from the working women's delegation should address the conference and ask Labour to help the cause. This request was never even submitted to the conference.[45]

*Roberts was often in demand as a speaker: this is Broughton, near Salford.*

A campaign was then mounted to heckle Labour leaders by the more militant Women's Social and Political Union. Roberts came off pretty well — he always flourished when being heckled, and in any case was firmly in favour of women's suffrage. On 26 February 1913 he addressed his constituents at the Agricultural Hall. After about twenty minutes a man in the audience called out 'What about the Franchise Bill?' He replied 'I regret that the Franchise Bill was destroyed, and that we have failed to secure the enfranchisement of women (Applause, and a female voice 'Did you try?'). I believe the claims of women to be based on justice and natural progress, and I do not think that you can ever deny to women the political power which is given to men'. The other Norwich MP, Low, was less of an enthusiast for women's suffrage. Whilst in favour of it in principle, according to his 1910 Election manifesto, he was not prepared to give it the highest priority

He suffered heckling at several meetings in Norwich in January 1914.

However, Roberts was opposed to militancy within the movement, as shown, for example, when he spoke at the Norwich Agricultural Hall on 26 February 1913. He said that he was committed to the struggle for the vote for women — including working women and married women — and if *Norwich Electors* did not want him to campaign for the women's vote, he would stop being their MP (cries of 'No, No' from the audience). However, he was strongly against militancy: 'I believe that reasoned, orderly methods are those alone which will appeal to the intellect in this or any other country (Applause). If I believed in the methods of violence, disorder and destruction I would be prepared to head the unemployed and ask

*Roberts speaking from a cart in Norfolk. George Edwards, farm workers' union leader, is far left.*

them to go out and destroy property. Because I do not adopt such methods you may take it from me I don't agree with them (Applause). Furthermore, I believe that in the ultimate they frustrate the legitimate aims of women or men. They provoke unnecessary hostility'.

The 'Cat and Mouse' Bill, which gave the Home Secretary power to release hunger strikers on licence and re-arrest them when they had recovered, came before Parliament in March 1913. Keir Hardie was strongly opposed to the Bill, but the Labour Members of Parliament were divided. In the end, seven of them voted against the Bill, but Roberts was one of the fourteen who voted in favour. The Bill was passed by a very large majority. He did not speak in the debate, but did make a contribution during the committee stage where the details of the Bill came under discussion. An amendment was proposed that the decision to release prisoners should be made by a High Court judge, rather than by the Home Secretary as the Bill proposed. Roberts opposed the amendment, pointing out that MP's could criticise decisions of the Home Secretary, whereas they had no power to comment on decisions made by judges. The amendment was withdrawn.

Roberts continued to put forward issues relevant to his own constituents. In June 1912, he raised the case of a man named George Ruthin who was in Norwich Castle gaol. Roberts asked if it was true Ruthin had 'been flogged with such severity as to tear pieces out of the man's back'. The Home Secretary replied that Ruthin had smashed all the furniture in his cell and had assaulted a prison officer. He had been given twelve strokes of the cat: 'it would be quite impossible to tear pieces out of the back with the instrument used: the skin was not broken'. Ruthin was transferred to Chelmsford gaol at his own request.

Roberts was obviously thinking of Norwich printers, of whom he was one by profession, when he asked in the House in July 1912 whether provincial firms could take on Government printing work, such as printing copies of the new National Insurance Act, on equal terms with printers in London. Norfolk suffered severely from flooding after a great rainstorm in August 1912. Roberts asked for Government help for reconstruction of bridges, and for Norfolk farmers and smallholders, and raised the issue of damage to housing stock in Norwich itself. He was told by John Burns that a loan had been given to repair bridges in the Erpingham district. As for Norwich itself, Burns thought the flooding was a good opportunity for the town council to 'take the matter of housing in hand': he would be happy to give the council assistance in the matter of loans.

In fact, Roberts' career nearly came to a premature end in October 1912. On 17 October, while at the House of Commons, he was suddenly taken ill and it was feared that he would not recover. For four days his condition was critical. Two days later it was reported that he was now 'taking nourishment well. His condition is still critical but there is hope that he may recover'. He was too ill to be moved from his hotel in Buckingham Street until 23 October when he was moved into a Nursing Home at St Thomas' Hospital. Three days later his health had improved slightly. In a debate in the House of Commons on 24 October, one MP, Dr Macnamara, referred to Roberts 'for whose speedy recovery from a serious illness we all hope'. By 30 October, he was on the road to recovery.[46]

However, it took him a couple of months to recover fully. On 26 November, it was noted in the House of Lords that a Bill on Norfolk Fisheries was being delayed because of his illness (he had been supporting objectors to the Bill). Fishing was clearly on his mind when his first contribution after his illness came in December. He raised the issue of the right of Lowestoft fishermen to shares of the profits of voyages.

He was sufficiently ɛ covered in December to be appointed to a Ro yal Commission to enquire into delays in the hearing of appeals to the High Court of Justice. It is perhaps a sign that he was still not very well known outside the Labour Party that *The Times* assumed the man appointed was C. H. Roberts (there was a Liberal M.P. of that name) rather than G. H. Roberts. A correction was issued and the Commission brought out its report in April the following year, recommending that the number of judges hearing High Court cases be increased.

The eighteen months after his recovery saw Roberts' finest speeches in the Commons, all on agricultural and land issues; it also saw his increasing divergence from his party on matters of defence.    Most Labour MPs were opposed to the rapidly increasing expenditure on the army and the navy in the years after 1906. However, they were not united on this. A small number, mainly with dockyards or armaments factories in their constituencies, voted for such increases as early as 1906. Roberts took a compromising line. He opposed the Army estimates in 1909 but recognised the need to keep the navy in 'a state of efficiency'. In 1910, although voting against the Navy estimates too, he agreed that it must be able to defend the nation, saying that 'we look upon the Navy as a form of national insurance, and the real difference between us is that we on these benches say that every pound spent in insurance premiums beyond what is actually necessary is a waste of national resources'.[47]

Roberts continued to take the Labour line on defence expenditure in 1911. He moved an amendment in Parliament declaring that an 'increase in expenditure on the Navy was not justified by foreign events and is a menace to peace and security'. He spoke on the issue at the 1911 Trades Union Congress:

> There is a scarcity of 100,000 houses in the rural districts, and the houses which do exist are certainly not fit habitation for decent human beings ... We should demand that some of the millions now squandered upon 'Dreadnoughts' should be spent in providing decent houses for the rural workers. This is a fundamental problem ... I have relatives of my own who cannot get their wants supplied in this direction.

In fact, Roberts was beginning to diverge from the official Labour Party in his view of the defence question. In spite of his position as Chief Whip, he was one of eight Labour MPs who rebelled against their party line by voting against a proposal to cut the money spent on re-arming the Navy in July 1912.[48]

However, Roberts was still campaigning eloquently for radical policies. In

February 1912, in a keynote speech in Parliament, he argued for a minimum wage, rejected the idea of tariff reform, and urged nationalisation of coal mines and railways. He continued to take a great interest in promoting the farm labourer and his conditions of work, repeatedly citing his own background in this area. Most of the other Labour Party Members of Parliament came from industrial and mining backgrounds, so it was easy for him to become the party 'expert' on agricultural issues. One of his best speeches in the Commons on the subject was on 13 March 1913, during a debate on a minimum wage. He began with his own story: 'I happen to come of agricultural stock, born in a small village in Norfolk'. He had seen that the Board of Trade figure for the average wage of a Norfolk farm labourer was 15 shillings a week. He said the figure was supplied by employers and was too high: 'I believe it is truer to say that the wages in the county of Norfolk average about 13 shillings a week. I am able to say that I have relatives of my own today in receipt of 12 shillings and 13 shillings a week.' Asked if this included extras, he was emphatic, returning to his own family: 'I am acquainted with cases in my own family where they simply have that wage without even a bit of garden ground; and they are forbidden to keep even a fowl or a pig to help them to eke out their existence.' He invited MPs to 'contemplate the life of the agricultural labourer'. His weekly expenses would be 2/- or 2s.6d. rent; 9d on clothes; 1s.6d on coal and light. A man with a wife and three children, even if he spent just one penny per person on each meal, would exhaust his entire weekly wage: 'You may say they will have to reduce the amount, but, even if they do, it must be realised even with that further reduction there is very little left for incidentals and the small luxuries which we believe ought to be the lot of every human being in this country'. In another speech, in February 1915, he quoted a relative working on a farm who received twelve shillings a week, from which rent was deducted, leaving just ten shillings. Once again, he stressed his personal experience: 'I have lived in these conditions, and gone and stayed with people who are subjected to these conditions'.

He gave another keynote speech in the Commons on 18 April 1913, this time summarising his views on rural housing:

> I have often stated in this House that I hope subsequently that the valuation of land which is now taking place shall be the basis of the subsequent acquisition of land for public purposes.
> I am less inclined as the years go by to dogmatise. I have been associated myself with a school of politicians who aver that all palliatives are valueless, and that after all we have to await the time when the working classes are of one mind, and then we are going to declare a social revolution and superimpose a perfect State on the

present imperfect order. I am one of those who have come to the conclusion that if I can do something of immediate avail, I do not care from what quarter it originates, it is going to have my hearty co-operation. I do not think I need waste time in relating the urgency and the extent of the problem.

I have spoken on previous occasions from the point of view of the agricultural labourer, because I am of him and I know the circumstances of his life. I have to recognise this. The agricultural labourer at the moment is unable to pay an economic rent. You may tell me that the raising of wages is the real solution. I do not attempt to deny it. The whole of our social legislation is due to the fact that some of our people do not get a fair share of wealth, and are unable to meet the responsibilities of life with the wage that they are able to win. The same argument which is advanced against State aid in this respect is equally applicable to all forms of social reform. So long as wages are regarded as simply sufficing for immediate need, you will have occasion for social reform. I constantly attempt to preach the principle in this way. The reward of labour should be regarded as sufficient to cover the whole liabilities of life, but nevertheless we have not yet reached that stage, and I cannot see any immediate prospect of that standard being established. Under the existing order, the daily wage simply suffices for the daily need, or the weekly wage for the weekly need, as the case may be. There must necessarily be a number of contingencies in life which cannot be properly met out of a wage fixed according to that standard ...

I spend some time among agricultural labourers, particularly in East Anglia, at different parts of the year. When the weather improves, I presume I will be using my week-ends addressing agricultural labourers. I find that a keen interest is being taken in this question. It is a vital matter. I know relatives who would have preferred to live in this country, but, being unable to get houses or to get married, they have been driven across the seas. I want to see our country entering into active competition with the Colonies. I view with grave apprehension the figures as to emigration which are placed before us now, and I believe that in the question of rural housing you have one of the most fruitful causes whereby people are driven away. When we have the startling fact that our emigration statistics reveal that we are sending out of the country year by year a number approximating to our natural increase of population, that seems to me to prove that, unless we are able to grapple with this subject, early stagnation must ensue, and an unfortunate state of deterioration enter into the life of our nation.

I find that rural life in this country is stagnant. I see the agricultural labourer housed under wretched conditions. I do not want to exaggerate at all. I know whole villages where the houses have not more than two bed-rooms, and the second one is a lean-to shanty. I say it would be almost impossible to exaggerate the evil effects of this condition of things.

On 27 May 1913, Roberts himself moved a Bill to regulate both wages and hours of farm labourers. He said that the average wage of a farm labourer in England was 17s.6d. a week, but this meant nothing because of the wide variation, from a much as 23 shillings a week where there was competition for labour from mining down to just 14 shillings a week; 'In the part of the land whence I hail, we are able to boast of the most fertile soil of the country, and yet rates of wages are the lowest in the land.' The answer was to introduce Agricultural Boards for each county to regulate conditions in its own region.

One week later, Prime Minister Asquith in effect killed Roberts' Bill: he announced that Government time could not be spared for its second reading. However, Roberts continued to promote the Bill. On Sunday 29 June, he spoke at an open air rally at Briston in Norfolk, organised by both railway and farmworkers' unions. He pointed out that he had introduced a Bill demanding a minimum wage for farm workers. This would be fixed by a local Board because of the great variation in farm wages in different parts of the country. The Bill would also introduce a maximum working week for farm labourers of fifty hours, including a statutory half day's holiday each week.[49]

Roberts took a great pride in his home city and its history. Even in a very busy year for him, he agreed to sit on a committee that organised events in Norwich to celebrate the centenary of the birth of one of the city's most famous writers George Borrow. However, he was unable to find the time to make much of a contribution and had to miss the event itself, held on 5 July 1913, due to political engagements elsewhere.

In the summer of 1913 he found himself involved in a dispute within the Labour Party concerning a forthcoming by-election in Leicester. He went to Leicester with Arthur Henderson to sort out an argument as to who should stand for Labour there. The problem was that Leicester, like Norwich, was a two-member seat, and, again like Norwich, Labour and the Liberals had each put up one candidate at the last general election. Both had been elected. As it happens the Labour MP was the party leader James Ramsay MacDonald. Now, in 1913, the Liberal victor had resigned for personal reasons and a by-election was due. Should Labour put up a candidate? Would not the Liberals see this as a breach of the Lib/Lab agreement, and start actively opposing Labour candidates? The Parliamentary Labour party could not forbid the local party to stand, it could only use its powers of persuasion. The local I.L.P. wanted to put up Alderman Banton, one of their prominent local men. Both Henderson and Roberts strongly urged them not to oppose the Liberal candidate. Although they were subjected to 'many angry interruptions' from Labour supporters they did eventually persuade the Party not to do so. However, another left-wing group, the British Socialist Party (B.S.P.), did put up a 'socialist' candidate.

The Labour Party were in a difficult position, especially as it seemed very likely that the Socialist would take enough votes from the Liberal candidate to allow the Conservatives to win. George Roberts played a key role in the by-election, and showed that willingness to converse with people of other parties that was later to cause him so much difficulty. He discussed the situation with a Liberal Leicestershire MP, Sir Michael Levy. Roberts leaked to him the fact that MacDonald wanted the B.S.P. candidate to do badly. Once this was revealed, the B.S.P. Liberals in Leicester put out a document purporting to be issued by the Labour Party and urging working men to support the Liberal candidate rather than the Socialist.

The by-election led to a furious and lengthy correspondence from the leading lights of the Norwich Labour Party in the columns of the *Eastern Daily Press*. Fred Henderson wrote:

> The position in which Mr Roberts has placed those who have hitherto been supporters seems to me to be quite an intolerable one. Through the person of our representative we figure, in the mind of the whole Socialist and Labour movement, as the one constituency responsible for betraying a Socialistic candidate for a furtive and despicable piece of too-clever-by-half political intrigue.[50]

However, two Norwich socialists, Frederick Crotch and Fred Easton, reminded readers of Henderson's own behaviour in the 1904 election, Easton adding 'Mr Henderson is adept at wrecking. Beware!' Holmes also supported Roberts, pointing out that the Socialist candidate in Leicester had expressed his desire to smash 'MacDonaldism'. He added 'I am sure that those who value Mr Roberts' past work and know that of his detractors will not hesitate one moment to place their belief in his honesty and straightforwardness, and his ability to give a reasonable explanation of the situation'. As it happened, the Liberal had an easy victory, and the Socialist finished bottom of the poll. Roberts was forced to apologise to the National Executive Committee of the Labour Party for his actions, but the affair blew over.

*Two caricatures of Roberts by 'Major'.*

*Roberts by 'Spy'.*

*Roberts as seen by J. E. Lunn.*

50

Robert's oratory was his greatest asset. He made perhaps his greatest Commons speech ever on the ownership of land on 29 April 1914. This included a clear statement of his thoughts:

> I believe the time is ripe for the State to make very large purchases of agricultural land. The demand for small holdings and the revival of agriculture seem to make this period particularly appropriate for a very large State venture of this character. I believe it is only by State ownership that you will ever be able to appropriate the social values which are created, not by individuals, but by the presence and industry of a population. I believe that our agricultural land is going to receive a very great increment in value in succeeding years. The growth of the population in all parts of the world, the present admitted restrictions of food supplies, the fact that the virgin qualities of the soil in our Colonies are already being exhausted, which means that great expenditure has to be devoted to the raising of crops, the use of more labour, and to expenditure on more manures and that sort of thing, are bound to increase the cost of producing the food supplies which have hitherto so plentifully flowed to these shores. I believe that is an inevitable world movement, and I am certain that we are reading the signs aright when we say that there is a very hopeful future for the agricultural industry of our country. At any rate, that is an opinion of my own, and I believe it is very widely shared by other thinkers in the community. That seems to me from a business point of view to afford a very strong reason why the State should not disregard the rural part of this problem, but should regard that as one of the most practicable and immediate means of realising the purpose of transferring land from private to public ownership. Of course, we are told that this will be a very expensive undertaking, and that we have no right to use public funds for this purpose. In my opinion, public money could not be devoted to a better purpose than bringing back the land of the country to the ownership of the country. We have spent light-heartedly, or at any rate freely, money on expensive expeditions in other parts of the world. I am not going to argue as to whether they were avoidable or justifiable, or what not, but if we had been able to avoid that form of wasteful expenditure and so have devoted £300,000,000 to the purpose of bringing our land back into the possession of the people, our country and our Empire would be much greater and better for our population than is the case at the present time.

He concluded: 'We believe that the land of every country ought to be the property of the people of that country.' This speech received high praise from Conservative MP Charles Bathurst, who wrote to Roberts: 'if you make many more of the same kind I shall feel bound to come across and sit on your benches'.[51]

In the event, however, it was Roberts, not Bathurst, who was to cross the floor of the House.

In early 1914, Roberts was involved in one of the most significant events in Norfolk before the war, the Burston School strike. This came about in April 1914, after Kitty and Tom Higdon were dismissed as teachers at Burston's county council school on largely trumped-up charges, but really because of their Christian Socialist views. Most of the children walked out of the school and continued to be taught by the Higdons, at first on the village green, then in temporary premises and finally in a purpose-built school in the village: the foundation stone for the new school was laid by George Lansbury in May 1917 in front of a very large crowd that included Sylvia Pankhurst. The school continued to function until Tom Higdon's death in September 1939, and the whole incident is sometimes known as 'the longest strike in history'. The affair is remembered today with an annual rally each September.

Higdon was involved in both the Independent Labour Party and the Agricultural Labourers' Union, and was a friend of Roberts, who had held a rally in Burston in 1913 in connection with his campaign on farm labourers' wages. Roberts was the first person to raise the issue of the school strike in Parliament. On 11 May 1914, he asked the President of the Board of Education if he was aware that the parents of Burston children had withdrawn them from the school as a protest against the dismissals, whether he had received an appeal for an enquiry, and whether he had come to a decision in the matter. The President replied that he was aware of the situation but did not intend to hold any enquiry into the matter.

# 3

# 'Democracy is doomed unless England is victorious': George Roberts, the War and after, 1914-1922

The Labour Party could be reasonably satisfied with its progress in Norwich by 1914. It had one MP, four city councillors and seven Guardians (these figures include three people who were both councillors and Guardians). The First World War was to change everything, including the relationship between the Party and its Member of Parliament.

The outbreak of war in August 1914 took people by surprise. Most people in England were in favour of it, especially after Germany invaded Belgium — the defence of 'gallant little Belgium' was a very popular rallying call. The Labour Party was split by the war. Its leader, Ramsay MacDonald, and members of one of its constituent parts, the Independent Labour Party, declared themselves against the war. However, most of the members of the Labour Party were in favour of the war, including George Roberts. In fact he played a key role in the final decision, as noted in *The Times* some years later:

> The story of the critical conferences of the Labour Party in the opening days of the war has never yet been published. When it is made known it will be found that Mr Roberts, at the start, stood almost alone in maintaining that it was the duty of Britain to enter the war on the side of France and Belgium. It was the greatest fight of his life, and he had the supreme satisfaction, after battling for long with his back to the wall, of seeing Mr Ramsay MacDonald and his pacifist friends driven out of the counsels of his party until the debt of honour for which he had contended had been paid in full.[52]

MacDonald resigned as leader of the Party and was replaced by Arthur Henderson. Broadly speaking, the division was between the trade unionists who were in favour of the war, and the members of the Independent Labour Party who opposed it. Several people like Roberts were in both camps, and, like him, they almost all came out in favour of the war. The majority of Labour MPs, including Roberts, favoured a Government request for a war credit of £100 million, and were even happy to help in the recruiting campaign. The I.L.P. opposed both these actions.

By coincidence, the I.L.P. held its annual conference in Norwich in 1915. The two main speakers were Keir Hardie and Ramsay MacDonald. Because of its anti-war stance, most Norwich meeting-places refused to stage the Conference. In the end a Primitive Methodist minister, Rev Storr, allowed them to use the schoolroom attached to his chapel in Queen's Road. The chairman of the Norwich Reception Committee was Herbert Witard and the treasurer was Annie Reeves. The Committee included Ernest Cornwell, later to serve a prison sentence for refusing to join up after conscription was introduced in 1916.

The I.L.P. conference issued a statement in April 1915: 'In each of the countries at war, the Militarist Jingoes declare that they will not rest content short of smashing and dismembering enemy countries. Even if such a policy, instead of setting at defiance the clearest lesson of history, were just and expedient, nine months of war under modern conditions have demonstrated that the possibility of attaining this result is exceedingly remote. But so long as this fear of dismemberment and crushing humiliation holds a nation in thrall, it will go on fighting to the last ounce of resistance and the last drop of blood'. Keir Hardie had been blunter: he said that the war consisted of 20 million working men trying to kill each other. The Conference passed a motion expressing its strong disapproval of Labour Party men taking part in recruiting campaigns and speaking on pro-war platforms. This was passed overwhelmingly, by a vote of 243 in favour, with just nine against. Roberts was in a tiny minority within the I.L.P., but in the Labour Party as a whole he was in the majority.

Roberts gave a speech at the 1915 T.U.C. explaining his reasons for his support of the war. Once again it was his own mind he had made up. He said that because he had been at first very much concerned about domestic matters, he had allowed the party and union leaders to make their decisions on foreign affairs. However, he and others had now looked at the matter themselves:

> Much as we regret it we have come to the conclusion that Germany meant war, that she had long planned it, and that she resorted to every device to create it, although perhaps not in the exact form in which it had ensued. She hoped for our neutrality. The hope was inspired in her breast that she might take her enemies one by one, because she would then find her purpose assured. After she had disposed of her other enemies then she would start upon her greater task — war with this country and the absorption of the British Empire.[53]

Roberts told the T.U.C., '... if there is murdering, maiming and a large number of killed, 96% of the wounded will be of our class. And, friends, we ought to honour these men'. He went on to describe his own experience: 'now, friends, if you want to know what war is, I have travelled 2,000 miles in France and Flanders, and I have seen the destruction of towns and villages. I have seen the spots where entire villages have been wiped out — where every man, woman and child has been killed. And let me tell you cynics that the German soldiers bayonetted the baby boys under the orders of their officers in order that they might never grow to manhood to avenge their parents' cold-blooded murder. I have seen them wait until the people were sitting down to meals, and then take pleasure in throwing a bomb to destroy the whole family circle. I have seen disembowelled bodies in a heap'.

To combat the anti-war views of the I.L.P., a pro-war Labour group, the Socialist National Defence Committee was formed in April 1915. Roberts was one of its founders. Others included George Barnes and the writer H. G. Wells. It was committed to 'ideals of liberty and democracy which have united free Britain, independent Belgium and Republican France'. After the sinking of the *Lusitania* in May 1915 the group called for the internment of Germans living in Britain. In 1916 the group was re-formed as the British Workers' League (B.W.L.). By the spring of 1917 it claimed to have 154 branches. Eleven of the 38 Labour Members of Parliament were at one time members, though some subsequently dropped out. Martin Pugh sums up: 'Militantly hostile to Asquithian Liberalism, conscientious objectors and German imports, the B.W.L. aligned itself with the fight-to-a-finish school.'[54] The group had contacts with pro-war Conservatives and there was even talk of a joint Tory-Socialist joint programme after the war. However, as war-weariness increased, many of the working class looked once more to the consistently anti-war stance of the I.L.P..

Low resigned as the 'other' Norwich MP due to ill health in January 1915. He wrote to Roberts: 'One of the greatest pleasures in representing Norwich has been having you as a colleague. We worked together well and I trust this spirit may long continue between those who sit for the old City irrespective of Party'. He was replaced by another Liberal, Edward Hilton Young, who was elected unopposed. He, too, got on well with Roberts over the ensuing years.

In January 1915, a Parliamentary Committee was formed to examine the conditions in which German prisoners of war and interned aliens were being held in Britain. Roberts was the Labour Party representative, and, as always, threw himself into his new role. He visited about twenty different camps between February and April, in England, Scotland and Ireland. These varied enormously in size and scope. Two of the largest were on the Isle of Man, where 5,000 interned aliens were held in huts at Knockaloe, near Peel, and a further 2,500 at a holiday camp in Douglas. Other camps holding between 1,800 and 2,000 prisoners were at Dorchester, Dorset (an old artillery barracks), Queensferry near Chester (a former engineering works), Leigh in Lancashire and Handforth in Cheshire. Several ships were also used, including three off Southend each holding about 1,500 men. Other institutions, especially those for officers, were much smaller. There were 100 Army and Navy officers at Donington Hall, 102, with 52 soldier-servants (themselves also prisoners of war) at Helport near Maidenhead, and 200 civilian prisoners at Lofthouse Park, Wakefield. The most dramatic moment in the inspections occurred at Helport, where the committee members were shown an escape passage that the prisoners had dug under a wall near the lavatories.

Roberts and the other members of the commission looked at conditions for themselves, and also heard complaints from the prisoners. Their criticisms were mainly relatively minor, the worst camp being Shrewsbury, where the sanitary arrangements were found to be 'very primitive'. Roberts himself wrote a letter, on House of Commons notepaper, urging that the situation be remedied; otherwise, he concluded, 'the Camp is excellently organised and administered'. The reports refer to camps several times as 'concentration camps', a term first used in the Boer War and one which had not yet acquired the full horror it was to have later in the century.

The only other serious concerns were at Handforth, an old dye works. Some prisoners shared double beds, which had led, according to the Commission, to 'immoral practices': these beds should be replaced with single ones. There was another issue at Handforth: there were about twenty to thirty Jews among the prisoners and there were no facilities there for catering for a Jewish diet. The complaints made by the prisoners themselves were also relatively trivial, mainly concerning the monotony of the food. One complaint was of the inadequacy of the butter supply, another that visitors were only allowed to talk for half an hour with a prisoner. This last complaint was at Wakefield where the civilian prisoners were visited by family and friends. Most of the military and naval prisoners would not have had anyone to visit them.

The final camp visited, on 30 April, was a rather different one, holding alien sailors and firemen. This was at Eastcote, Northamptonshire, in a house which had been bought by the British Sailors' and Firemen's Union, and fitted up at a cost to them of £10,000. It was not a prisoner-of-war camp, the prisoners being put on their honour not to escape. If they did try they would be sent to a military camp.[55]

On 25 February 1915, there was a debate in Parliament about allowing children in country districts to leave school before the statutory leaving age of thirteen to work on the land. Roberts spoke at length, vigorously opposing the proposal. He made his usual references to his agricultural background: 'I happen to be one of those born in a small agricultural village who still maintain a pretty intimate interest with conditions there prevailing ... I am myself of agricultural descent, and therefore I am not likely to hold or acknowledge that there is a law that dooms a child born of rural parents to a less finely convoluted brain than a child born in town'. He cited the case of a relative who lived in the country who as a young man had been forced to go out poaching to raise money for botany books. Despite his lack of formal education, he had done very well on emigrating: '... this all goes to emphasise the fact that there be much genius latent among the agricultural population, and much talent which, if released, will redound to the benefit of the country as a whole'.

Henry Chaplin, MP for Wimbledon, and a former President of the Board of Agriculture, showered Roberts with, perhaps sardonic, praise — and then went on to disagree totally with his views. In his tribute, he praised Roberts for 'the progress which the Hon Gentleman has made from a lowly beginning in a cottage until he has been able, by his latent genius, to raise himself to the proud and responsible position which he now occupies as a representative of labour in this House ... I congratulate him on the possession of those qualities which have enabled him to reach his present position'. In fact, Roberts was about to rise to further heights.

By the spring of 1915, many people were becoming dissatisfied with the conduct of the war. The Liberal government, under its rather alcoholic leader Asquith, was thought to be insufficiently dynamic to win the war. In May 1915, he was forced to bring Conservative and Labour Party members into a coalition government. Arthur Henderson, the leader of the Labour Party, came into the Cabinet. Two other Labour MPs came into the Government in lesser positions. These junior ministers included Roberts, who was appointed a Junior Lord of the Treasury. (The third Labour man to join the government was William Brace, who was not one of the original 29 that formed the Parliamentary Labour Party: he had been elected as a 'Lib-Lab' and only moved into the Labour Party later).

Just nine years after its foundation, the Parliamentary Labour Party had members in the Government, and Roberts was one of them! A Liberal MP, William Wedgewood Benn, wrote him a letter of congratulation, but also issued a warning: 'I hope you are keeping well and not overworking — which always seemed to me your danger'.

Roberts was certainly not about to slow down. He did valuable work for the Government as a pro-war trade unionist. He was involved in the negotiations that ended the South Wales miners' strike in July 1915. He and Arthur Henderson, as

SATURDAY, JUNE 26, 1915.

## ON THE TREASURY BENCH.

*The Independent (a trade union newspaper) — The Treasury Front Bench 1915, Roberts on the right.*

leaders of 'labour' put Lloyd George's 'final' terms to the miners' leaders on 1 July They were rejected and two weeks later 200,000 miners were on strike. Welsh coal was needed to fuel the British fleet so Lloyd George eventually gave in to the miners' demands. In this way he undermined Roberts and Henderson, whose 'final' offer turned out not to be final after all.

Roberts also became the face of pro-war Labour in Europe, visiting France on at least four occasions in the last three months of 1915. He wrote these experience up in *The Typographical Circular*. He explained these visits in his own words: 'I has been desired by certain French and British Socialists and Labourists that visit Paris there to explain before a representative assembly the part played b the war in this country. This because a few British newspapers have disparage and belittled the national effort; and because the speeches and writings of certai of our pacifists have tended to misrepresent the attitude of our working classes These two elements have created a widespread impression that our people are either indifferent or opposed to a whole-hearted support of the Allies' cause... To present matters in proper proportion was the mission I was called upon to fulfil.' Naturally his accounts stress the positive aspect of his visits, with passing soldiers shouting their support. Once, on a Paris railway station, 'As I walked along the platform I was greeted by a group of British soldiers with shouts of 'Good old George!' Hats were thrown in the air and cheering was sustained.' On one occasion he spoke to a conference at Bordeaux attended by more than 1,500 people. He also toured docks and armaments factories.[56]

By the summer of 1915 it was becoming clear that conscription would eventually be introduced. This caused further splits in the Labour Party — many people who were prepared to support the war would not support forcible call-ups of unwilling men. Roberts was in no doubt. He was convinced that conscription was necessary to win the war. He was one of several Labour leaders who publicly declared that they would be willing to consider conscription if the Government thought it was essential while official Labour party policy was to oppose conscription. George Barnes also supported conscription even though he had paid the ultimate price of war. His son Henry had been killed on the Western Front in 1915. At a local level, Fred Henderson also supported conscription: he wrote a letter to *The Times* to say so.

The annual Labour Party Conference was held at Bristol early in 1916: here the I.L.P. delegates were just an element within the whole party. James Sexton of the Transport Workers Union put forward a motion declaring that the Government was fully justified i n t he w ar a nd p ledging t he C onference t o s upport t he Government in the successful prosecution of the war. Ramsay MacDonald spoke against the war. He was opposed by Roberts who described the speech as 'ostrich-like'. The *Daily Herald* commented on Roberts' speech: 'His reception was far from cordial, but with considerable dexterity he managed to get a good hearing...It was perhaps foolish of him to declare that every vote cast against the motion was in effect a vote for the Germans, for, if that is so, no less than 600,000 Trade Unionists[57] are against the war'.[58]

The Conference did indeed support the war by 1,502,000 votes to 602,000. Labour was supporting Roberts' stand. The Conference did pass a vote against conscription, but it also resolved that Roberts and the other Labour Party ministers should stay in government even after conscription had been introduced.

Perhaps it was Roberts' stories of childhood that prompted a Mrs Manning, a housekeeper in Devonshire Street, London, to beg him for financial help. She had run into problems, she claimed, when not only had she lost a sovereign out of her purse, but her little girl had thrown a pound note onto the fire! She pleaded: 'the thought of my seven children drives me to try and find a friend just for a few days'. Roberts sent her two pound notes as a loan, but perhaps he was too optimistic in expecting its return. Mrs Manning wrote again, saying she had hoped to send him one pound back, but, even though she was now taking in washing, it was very hard to struggle on her wages with so many children,

*Henderson and Roberts at the Hotel Continental, Paris, 30 December 1916. Behind, the official interpreter (with beard) and the two men's secretaries.*

especially as her daughter was remarkabl careless with money. This time she had los a one-pound note belonging to a woma for whom she ran errands! There is n more correspondence, so it is not known Roberts ever got his money back.

In July 1916, the Norwich branch of th No Conscription Fellowship asked Robert what steps he would take to remedy th Tribunal system. He said that he though it did not need any remedy as it was a fai system. The *Daily Herald* was sarcastic: '.. he could not pledge himself to advocat the immediate release of objector pending a new Government order ... Stil this great, just man did not suggest tha COs [conscientious objectors] and thei families should be given a term in boilin oil or condemned to read the speeches o Labour leaders in office. They must feel relieved and grateful!'[59]

In December 1916, there was a successful plot by the Conservative and some Liberal leaders to replace Asquith with Lloyd George, who was see as a much more charismatic leader. The Labour Party was a minor playe but it had to be represented in the new Government too. Roberts wa again one of their ministers, becoming Parliamentary Secretary to th Board of Trade. One of the problems that arose during the war was that o keeping the workers at home from going on strike in an age of rising prices Lloyd George created a new ministry, the Ministry of Labour. As a believe in 'horses for courses' he thought that this position could best be filled b members of the Labour Party. The first Minister of Labour was Roberts' frien John Hodge. The *Daily Herald* was cynical, saying that Hodge's functio would be to 'force or persuade the Labour movement to accept th policies produced by the various capitalist departments'.[60]

In April 1917, a Corn Production Bill came before the House o Commons. It was of special interest to Roberts, with his Norfol agricultural background. Walter Runciman, a former President o the Board of Trade specifically mentioned Norfolk in his speech i the debate. Roberts stood up, saying he had not planned to speak, an then launched into one of his most impassioned speeches. He said tha no-one knew how long the war might go on, and said that he now though you could not rely on the industry to develop naturally without Stat intervention, saying that: 'because of that fact my views have undergone great changes', at which other MPs called out 'Hear, Hear'. He continued, 'I understand the faculty of common sense to see things as they are. I have endeavoured during the years that I have been in this House to face problems in a practical fashion. I have associated myself with hon. Members irrespective of Party.'

He thought that if men were to be attracted to the land after the War, conditions for farm labourers must be improved: 'I have been, and still am, a labour agitator. Throughout my life I have urged that the class to which I belong is entitled to better wages and improved conditions.' He thought that it would be several generations before agriculture could be profitable. When an MP intervened to ask

*Henderson and Roberts featured on the front cover of L'Image de la Guerre, a French pro-war publication.*

if he did not mean 'years' rather than 'generations', he responded: 'I am a very modest little chap'. Lloyd George wrote to him on the following day praising this speech: 'Congratulations on your conspicuous Parliamentary success yesterday. It was fine and has given great pleasure to all your friends.'[61]

On 31 December 1916 James Hogge, a Scottish MP, had queried Roberts, in his Board of Trade role, how it was that soldiers landing at Aberdeen for a period of leave had found themselves trapped there because of a failure in the train service. Hogge added pointedly, 'Does the hon. Gentleman know what a punishment it is to spend a weekend at Aberdeen?' Within a year, Roberts was to find out!

Divisions about the war within the Labour Party led to a farce in the summer of 1917. The Labour Party Executive decided that the Party should not attend the International Conference of Socialists in Stockholm. Instead they would send delegates to Russia to invite delegates from that country to a conference of Allied Socialist parties to be held in London. They chose Henderson, Roberts and a trade unionist representative for the journey. At the last moment MacDonald decided that he wanted to go too. Cabinet met on 23 May 1917. It resolved that MacDonald could go with two colleagues, but that Roberts should also go as head of a delegation 'of the majority section of the British Labour Party'. MacDonald and his friends jostled for places on the train to Aberdeen while 'George Roberts, as befitted a minister in the Coalition Government, took a separate compartment'.[62]

At Aberdeen they were intercepted by 'Captain' Tupper, of the Seamen's and Firemen's Union, a strongly pro-war man. He refused to allow the crew of the ship to sail. The Labour men had arrived on the morning of 10 June. They waited all day on board ship for something to happen. Roberts attended a meeting of the seamen's union, where he was introduced by Tupper as 'a proved friend of labour and especially of seamen'. Roberts appealed to the seamen to allow the delegation to continue, trying to earn their support saying that he was planning to raise the issue of compensation for the dependants of seamen killed in the war. His appeal was in vain. On the afternoon of the following day, Roberts was called back to London. The others still waited!

In fact, there were to be serious consequences. Henderson went to Paris with Ramsay MacDonald to discuss the Stockholm Conference with French Socialists. Lloyd George thought this was a betrayal of the war cause by Henderson and sacked him from his inner War Cabinet. He was replaced by George Barnes, Minister of Pensions, and a close friend of Roberts. Hodge was moved from Labour to Pensions, and Lloyd George then made Roberts himself Minister of Labour in August 1917. This was to be a pinnacle of Roberts' career. The son of a village shoemaker had achieved the rank of a departmental minister in His Majesty's Government. *The Times* noted that Roberts had 'taken most of the Parliamentary burden of the Department' and had been for some time marked out for promotion. The President of the Board of Trade, Arthur Stanley, was sorry to lose him:

> We have not been together many months but it has been long enough for me to have appreciated your many admirable qualities and to have formed an attachment to you which I shall always treasure. You will be a great success as Minister of Labour.[63]

Roberts was promoted to the highest councils of the land, being made a Privy Councillor. Lloyd George was really ruling through a small War Cabinet of half a dozen, but other 'outer Cabinet' ministers attended as needed. Roberts was in a bind on 20 August, just three days after his appointment. The subject under discussion was the Corn Production Bill, to which the House of Lords had introduced some minor amendments. Roberts was able to inform the other ministers that although the amendments were not very important, he was certain that they would be opposed by Labour MPs. The War Cabinet decided to invite the Commons to reject these amendments. Just six days later, a secret Cabinet memorandum about employment exchanges and the role of the Ministry of Labour commented that 'Mr Roberts arguments [unspecified] are very strong'.

Roberts was making his presence felt within the top levels of Government.

The actual swearing in as Privy Councillor took place at Buckingham Palace on 22 August 1917. He was sent instruction which would have been distasteful to some of his former Labour colleagues: 'Take the oath of allegiance kneeling (right knee) and then in proper order move forward to kiss the King's hand, again kneeling (right knee).' Roberts was moving well away from his Socialist roots. Five years later, when a French newspaper mistakenly referred to him as 'Lord' Roberts, he joked how shocked his former friends would be on hearing of his promotion!

Traditionally, when an MP received an appointment to such high office, he submitted himself to a by-election to secure the approval of his constituents. There were some precedents for not doing this, but Roberts decided to go ahead and a by-election was announced. The Conservative and Liberal Parties, as part of the Coalition, said that they would not run candidates. The question was whether the anti-war elements in the Norwich Labour Party would put up a man against him. Roberts was defiant:

> I am confident of the prospects if there is a fight. There is absolutely no doubt that the great body of labour opinion is in favour of carrying the war to a successful conclusion. Democracy is doomed unless England is victorious.

The National Executive of the Labour Party had a pro-war majority and naturally endorsed Roberts. The Independent Labour Party in Norwich was divided, but the majority of its members were anti-war — Witard estimated that they were three to one against Roberts. When the Representative Committee met, Roberts' union, the Typographical Association, moved that he be nominated. A member of the Boot and Shoe Operatives moved that he be repudiated. Witard objected to Roberts' attitude on Labour questions, especially his failure to vote for a recent Labour amendment to secure a minimum wage of 30 shillings a week for farm labourers. Fred Jex was blunter: 'this Council has been opposed to Roberts' war policy for three years'. Witard's forecast was proved correct: the vote was 41 to 14 against nominating Roberts. He was thus de-selected by his own party, and has the dubious honour of being the Labour Party's first ever de-selection.

Roberts then announced that he would stand as an Independent. He held a meeting at the Agricultural Hall on 24 August, the day before nominations were due to close. His friend and Labour Party colleague George Barnes, glorying in his new status as a member of Lloyd George's inner War Cabinet, came to Norwich to support him. Roberts was in a bombastic mood: he said that his 'friends' in Norwich who were now opposing him 'would be doing far greater justice to themselves if they were engaged in entering protests against the rape of Belgium, the sinking of the *Lusitania*, the murder of Nurse Cavell and Captain Fryatt'. Roberts was loudly cheered when he said that he was quite ready, when this storm had passed, to have his work for the agricultural labourer compared with that of any other member of the Labour or Socialist party. *The Times* reported that a letter of support for Roberts had been sent by 43 men serving on the front line. They urged their relatives in the city to give him their votes.[64]

Roberts printed a rejoinder to the attacks upon him, which he analysed as being threefold:

1. That he had helped to pass the Munitions Act. His reply was that the trades unions concerned had been involved in drafting the Act — and, in any case, he had actually abstained in the vote!

2. That he supported the Military Service Act. He asked his opponents a direct question: 'Does their resistance to any form of recruitment mean that they prefer the defeat of their country to the subordination of their doctrines to national ends? The citizens of Norwich are entitled to a straightforward reply to this question.'

3. His vote on the minimum wage for farm labourers in the committee stage of the Corn Production Bill. The Labour Party had wanted this to be fixed at thirty shillings a week, but Roberts had voted for twenty five shillings. He said that this was because the higher figure would never have got through Parliament, so that the whole Bill would have collapsed unless the compromise figure was accepted.

In spite of the bitter feelings aroused among Labour Party members in Norwich, there was no by-election campaign. No 'peace' candidate came forward and Roberts was elected unopposed on 25 August. James Homes, Organising Secretary of the National Union of Railwaymen, wrote to congratulate him:

> My very warmest congratulations at your unopposed return for Norwich, in a sence (*sic*) I was sorry the Condensed Milk Group had not the courage to fight, they would have been wiped out, they evidently knew that.

In October 1917 Roberts was asked to leave the local branch of the I.L.P.. The secretary, W. Maxey, wrote to him:

> Doubtless you are aware that a vast amount of difference has existed between the local branch and yourself for some time past and the climax to such difference was made manifest a short time ago when the Local Movement repudiated your candidature at the recent Bye-election at Norwich.

*Roberts receives the Freedom of Norwich at Saint Andrew's Hall.*

In his reply Roberts said that he was being asked to resign 'owing to differences on war questions between some members of the branch and myself'. He pointed out that he had been a member of the branch for 'about 22 years', and he doubted if the majority of the I.L.P. branch members would agree with the decision. However, he accepted his dismissal with fairly good grace.[65]

Norwich as a city still loved him. As one of the few Norwich MPs to achieve high government office, he was presented with the freedom of the city on 10 May 1918. The freedom was given to him by the Lord Mayor of the time, Richard Jewson. Jewson said: 'no dual constituency ever in war-time had two braver men to represent them — one in the political arena, the other on the battlefield'. This reference was to Hilton Young, who had fought in the naval raid at Zeebrugge just two weeks earlier. Although wounded in the arm he had continued on deck: as a result he had lost the arm.

Henderson's dismissal from office in 1917 was a blessing in disguise for Labour. He set about the re-organisation of the party. Until this date it was not possible for an individual to be a member of the Labour Party: you had to join one of its constituent elements, most commonly the I.L.P.. Now you could join as an individual. In the long run this was the death knell of the I.L.P. as it was no longer relevant: however it was still to be a force for another fifteen years. Henderson

*Roberts lighting No. 9 furnace at Stanton Ironworks Company, Derbyshire, 20 October 1917.*

also announced that he would never again join a government in which Labour did not predominate. The 'Lib-Lab' pact was formally over. Both were now fully independent political parties, equally opposed to the Conservative Party and to each other.

The Labour Party Conference for 1918 was held at Nottingham in January. As before, the party was divided, but the majority of its members supported the war. Several resolutions urged that Labour Party men should withdraw from the Government, but these were defeated. Two resolutions criticised the Executive of the Party for supporting Roberts at the by-election. The most virulent, from Great Yarmouth and District Trades and Labour Council, urged that 'necessary steps be taken to prevent Mr Roberts having membership of the Parliamentary Labour Party'. These views were those of a minority within the party and the resolutions were not passed.

Roberts was still very much a trade union man. He was instrumental in the struggle to increase the wages in the building trades in Norwich. This resulted in a rise of two pence an hour in September 1917. In February 1918 he was able to exclude the boot and shoe industry from the operations of the Unemployment Insurance acts, which earned him a grateful letter from the General Secretary of the National Union of Boot and Shoe Operatives. In March 1918, Wakefield Trades Council invited him to stand as 'Labour Democratic' candidate for Wakefield. Roberts preferred to take his chances in his home city:

> Having represented the City of Norwich in Parliament for twelve years, and believing that I retain the confidence of a majority of the electors in that constituency, I have decided to appeal to them for the support necessary to continue my Parliamentary career. Whilst it would be a great honour to represent Wakefield, I am particularly proud of the fact that my fellow-citizens should have sent me to Parliament, and appear willing to renew their confidence in me.[66]

In May 1918 the Government were under pressure because of German advances on the Western Front. It was decided to extend industrial compulsion schemes. Roberts was in favour, provided 'only moral pressure was used to secure enrolment'. He urged that 'nothing should be done which would throw the trade unions into opposition'. He wanted the Trade Union Advisory Committee to be consulted.[67]

In the summer of 1918 the Labour Party decided to withdraw its support for Lloyd George's coalition. This was a crisis for the Labour ministers in the Government. They had a straightforward choice: stay in government and leave the Labour Party, or leave the government and stay in the party. Some left the government, including Roberts' friend John Hodge. Four ministers decided to break with the Labour Party and stay in the Government. They were George Barnes, James Parker, George Wardle — and George Roberts.

At the 1918 Trades Union Congress, Roberts spoke against peace negotiations being discussed at the International Conference. G. Sanders of the Licensed Vehicle Workers called out 'You get £2,000 a year to talk like that'. Roberts replied 'I get £2,000 a year it is true, but I should have thought you would have been glad that the position relating to the salary was occupied by a man of your own class'. Sanders 'retorted with a further personal reference reflecting upon the public character of Mr Roberts', for which the President rebuked him.

The Labour Party in Norwich disowned Roberts in the summer of 1918. However, by no means all working men agreed with their decision. Many union men supported Roberts. The local branch of the Typographical Association — who had paid Roberts' wages from the time he was elected in 1906 until MPs began to be paid in 1912 — were still in support. They said that they thought that Roberts was conforming to the National Labour Party view. It was Witard, with his anti-war stance, who was going against the opinion of the National Party. They added that Roberts' views on the war represented those of the majority of trade

*Roberts at war: Norwich Tank Week, 1918.*

unionists. T. F. Richards, General President of the Boot and Shoe Operatives, wrote to Roberts in June:

> So very sorry to see that the men you have so nobly and loyally served should prove more base than the Employing class.[68]

*Roberts in 1919 speaks about the Victory Loan scheme outside Norwich Guildhall.*

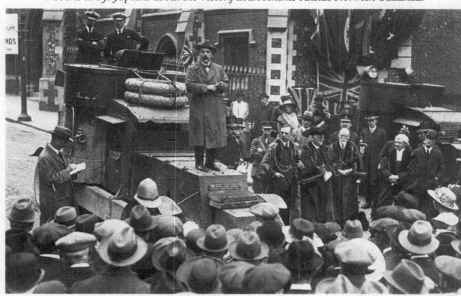

## 'Democracy is doomed unless England is victorious'

On 12 July 1918 Roberts made his first speech since the Labour Party had repudiated him. He spoke at the Electric Theatre in Norwich and supported the further calls made by the Government on manpower:

> I would not have it on my conscience that there is any one man in our Army or in the allied armies whose life I could have saved, but I know that we must furnish more and more men: because the more men we are able to send the less loss of life will be encountered in the remaining stages of this conflict.

The fighting ended with the Armistice on 11 November 1918. Lloyd George decided to hold a quick election in December. This election could be regarded as the first democratic election in Britain. All women over 30 could now vote for the first time — and so could about 5 million men aged over 21 previously debarred because they did not have a residence qualification. The electorate almost tripled in number, to about 22 million people — almost 13 million men and 8.5 million women. It is fascinating to consider what effect this great expansion of the electorate would have had in a 'normal' general election. However the 1918 election was anything but normal. Lloyd George wanted to continue in power at the head of the coalition that had supported him during the war. He gave each supporter of his coalition a letter, signed by both himself and the Conservative leader Andrew Bonar Law, urging the electors to vote for the candidate. Asquith, with wartime ration books in mind, referred to this letter as a 'coupon', and the election has become known as the coupon election.

In Norwich, Roberts and the Liberal Hilton Young were both supporters of Lloyd George. Young was still in north Russia fighting the Bolsheviks when the election was called. Roberts stood under the title 'Coalition Labour'. Their only opponent was an official Labour candidate, the anti-war campaigner Herbert Witard. He had to face heckling from ex-soldiers and other supporters of the war, and even received death threats. He calmly responded that he had been fighting for the workers' cause for 25 years and was not going to flinch now.[69]

In his election address, Roberts took pride in his war record and emphasised the need for natural unity:

> Throughout the war I have co-operated heartily in the measures which were proved necessary for its prosecution, and which have enabled Great Britain and the Allied nations to achieve Peace through Victory. This glorious result was made possible, in my opinion, only because of the splendid unity which has characterised the nation during the four years of this great world conflict. Now

that an armistice has been signed and a good peace seems certain, the nation is confronted with the task of demobilisation and re-settlement, connected with which are problems more difficult and complex than any that emerged during hostilities. At this juncture it appears to me desirable that controversy should be avoided as far as practicable, and that all should concentrate on maintaining an atmosphere of good will and on the carrying out of the many schemes requisite for the restoration of society to a peace basis. The work of reconstruction is beyond the capacity of a single party: its character, its complexities, its magnitude, require the effort of the whole people. Holding this view, I have decided to stand at this election as a Labour Coalition Candidate.

In the country as a whole, coupon and other pro-war candidates had an overwhelming success. Norwich was no exception:

**General Election 1918:**

| ROBERTS (Coalition Labour) | 26,642 |
| HILTON YOUNG (Coalition Liberal) | 25,555 |
| Witard (Labour) | 6,856 |

The head of the *Norfolk News Company* appreciated what Roberts had achieved:

It must be a source of satisfaction to you that you have not only carried the Liberal and Unionist vote but an overwhelming proportion of the Labour vote as well. It is a vote of confidence in yourself and in the policy you have pursued through the war.[70]

George Roberts was in Parliament for another term, with prospects of a further spell in high office.

# 4

# 'Free of all political parties' George Roberts in Parliament, 1918-1923

## The national scene

Lloyd George's Coalition had an enormous majority in Parliament. It was made up of 339 Coalition Conservatives, 134 Coalition Liberals and just four Coalition Labour men. The Coalition was thus dominated by Conservatives but under the premiership of a Liberal, Lloyd George. The opposition parties were miniscule: there were 59 Labour MPs (up from 39 before the war), and 26 Independent Liberals. There were also 73 Sinn Fenians representing Irish seats, but they refused to come to Westminster. .

George Roberts was one of the four former Labour Party men who preferred power in the Coalition government to the opposition benches. He was appointed Minister of Food Control, or Food Controller as he was commonly called, in January 1919. At first he declined Lloyd George's offer of this post, but the Prime Minister was not used to being thwarted and persuaded Roberts to take the job.[71]

The post had been created in 1916, and had been of key importance in the war, responsible for the voluntary and, in the last months of the war, compulsory, control and rationing of the nation's food supplies. However, these problems did not disappear as soon as the war ended. Difficulties of supply continued for another year. Even so, The Times expressed surprise at the appointment, noting that Roberts was leaving a ministry 'at which he has done well' for one 'the functions of which must be of diminishing importance'.[72]

Roberts attended Cabinet on 24 January 1919, when it discussed the price and strength of beer. He thought that 'a substantial reduction in the price and an increase in the supply would have a good effect on public opinion and do much to allay the prevailing unrest'. In this he was echoing his more senior colleague, Andrew Bonar Law, who at the same meeting said 'many people attributed the present unrest to the lack and poor quality of beer'. Cabinet resolved to increase the quantity of beer available by 25% and increase the maximum permitted strength.

3rd January, 1919.

My dear Labour Minister,

In view of the recent general election and of the termination of the war, I have advised the King that a reconstruction of the Government is necessary, and His Majesty has given his assent.

I should be greatly obliged if you would place your resignation in my hands in order to enable me to submit the names of a new Ministry to the King.

Ever sincerely,

Rt. Hon. G. H. Roberts, M.P.,
Minister of Labour.

Roberts was in his place on the Government front bench when Parliament opened on 4 February 1919, facing his former Labour Party colleagues, now in opposition. His position must have seemed even more significant as Lloyd George himself and two Cabinet colleagues, Arthur Bonar Law and George Barnes, were in France taking part in the Versailles Conference to thrash out peace terms after the war. Ten days later he was included in a Cabinet committee to investigate food prices with a view to securing reductions as soon as possible. Roberts had been specifically asked by Lloyd George to try to keep food prices down and in the first months this appeared to be working. However, later in the year prices rose once more due mainly to international factors, particularly the fall in the value of the pound in the United States.

Roberts was always keen to stamp his personality on any office he held, and soon produced a 'Statement of Policy' for his department. It began:

> Government Control: The policy of the Ministry is to consider control and de-control from the standpoint of price. If, in our opinion, the abandonment of control will result in a reduction of prices, we will de-control. If there is danger of prices remaining at their present level or rising above it, we are going to retain control'.

He went on to apply this to specific products. For beer, he was able to reprise the recent Cabinet debate: 'It is constantly being represented to us from Labour and other organisations that the shortage of beer and spirits is a cause contributing to the unrest in the country. I hope very shortly to be in a position to allow a considerably larger output of beer and of better quality [by which he meant stronger!] than that recently sanctioned'.

He was hoping also to arrange for some increase in the quantity of spirit available, especially as he thought it conducive to health: 'One could not fail to be in sympathy with the public demand for more spirits at this time, when influenz is rampant'. He was unable to offer immediate relief as to the price of wheat, but had better news on cheese and fish. He was hoping to announce a reduction in the price of cheese within a few days while white fish was being decontrolled entirely.

There were two aspects of the work of his Ministry that he thought it important to continue, even if the Ministry itself were to be abolished — milk and 'national kitchens'. On milk, he was forthright: 'In my view, Government control is necessary to secure increased milk supplies under guaranteed prices to improve the quality of milk, to prevent the domination of the trade by trusts, to effect economies in the wholesale and retail distribution of milk, and to ensure its equitable distribution'. National kitchens were a policy put forward by his predecessor as Minister of Food, J. R. Clynes, now back in the Labour Party ranks on the Opposition Bench. Roberts concurred with Clynes that national kitchens 'should become a permanent feature of our national life'. He added: 'It seems to be particularly needed in industrial areas, where cheap wholesome food is not under present conditions by any means always easily obtainable'.

Roberts concluded his policy statement with some general remarks, showing that he was aware that his Ministry was probably not a permanent institution:

> My policy, shortly, is this: - Control or decontrol, whichever will bring about lower prices. For example, we continue to control sugar, because our selling price for that

10

9th January, 1919.

My dear Roberts,

In reconstructing the Government I am finding, as you can well understand, great difficulty in allotting the different offices. In making these changes the arrangement which seems to me best is that you should take Mr. Clynes' place at the Food Ministry and I shall be much obliged if you will accept that office. I have come to the conclusion that it will not be possible to continue, now that the war is

is practically over, the arrangement about pooling which was made during the war and I therefore much regret that for the time being at least this will necessitate a disadvantage as compared with your pecuniary position in the late Government.

Yours sincerely,

10th January, 1919.

My dear Prime Minister,

I have your letter suggesting that I should take Mr. Clynes' place at the Ministry of Food. While I thank you for offering me this appointment I regret that with all respect I must decline to accept it.

Yours sincerely,

The Rt.Hon. D. Lloyd George, M.P.,
12, Downing Street,
S.W.1.

commodity is lower than the world's market price. We are ceasing to control tea and margarine because we have ample stocks, and believe that the free flow of competition will bring about an immediate fall in retail prices.

I think everybody regards the Ministry of Food as not being one of the permanent Departments of the State, but experience has proved that certain forms of control ought to be preserved permanently. We are now engaged in considering these matters. We feel that certain powers now exercisable under the Defence of the Realm Act should be incorporated in permanent form, and we are drafting a Bill with a view to giving continuity to that policy. If the work of the Ministry declines to a point which seems to us not to warrant the retention of a definite Department with a large staff and all its administrative cost, the work, which, in our opinion, should remain will be divided up amongst other Departments. Some might go to the new Ministry of Supply; some perhaps to the Board of Trade.

Tireless as ever, Roberts found time to attend the Peace Conference at Versailles: his pass to go survives among his papers at the Norfolk Record Office. There in his capacity of Food Controller, naturally he was only a very minor player, principally acting in support of his colleague, George Barnes. Barnes attended the Conference as the government's Labour Representative, and led the way in the discussions which resulted in Article XIII of the Peace Treaty, setting up the Organisation of Labour as part of the League of Nations. Barnes was one of five British statesmen to actually sign the Versailles treaty. Roberts had a smaller role, taking part in the discussions which led to the nine labour principles incorporated in article 427. These included the right of association by employees and the principle that men and women should receive equal pay for equal work. He would undoubtedly have approved of these, and no doubt enjoyed socialising with the delegates: he would have known many of the French representatives from his wartime visits to Paris.

However, it was the Ministry that was his main concern. As late as September 1919, he wrote:

The Ministry of Food is doing everything possible to eliminate the profiteer, while allowing reasonable profits to producers and traders. For this reason control, which most people had hoped to see removed, is being continued during the approaching winter ... I am not concerned so much about supplies as about high prices.[74]

General opinion was that Roberts was doing a very good job in difficult circumstances. A letter to Roberts from Walter Long survives among Roberts' papers at the Norfolk Record Office. Long was one of the leading figures in the Conservative Party at the time and was also a member of Lloyd George's coalition government. In October 1919 he wrote:

> At the risk of making you smile I really must congratulate you upon the wonderful smoothness and success with which your Food system has worked. Everybody is talking about it... Of course you won't answer.[74]

In fact, Roberts was no longer as opposed to Long's way of thinking as the final sentence of Long's letter had implied. During 1919, Roberts' views moved decisively to the right. There was a great deal of discontent during the year as soldiers returned to find high prices and few jobs. There were many strikes and a good many reasonable people feared that revolution would break out. Many people thought that Russian Bolsheviks were behind the unrest. Roberts took this line: he was still a convinced trade unionist, but thought that unions were in danger of being taken over by people who favoured revolution. In a speech at the Savage Club on 1 April 1919 he linked these revolutionaries with anti-war leaders:

> Some professed to be ready for a great revolution. Many of those who describe themselves as pacifists and whose conscience was so alive that it would not allow them to take part in shedding blood, were those who now talked most freely of manning barricades and turning machine guns on men of their own race who happened to belong to a different class from themselves.[75]

Speaking at Great Yarmouth on 2 July, Roberts said that the cost of living would only go down if national wealth was stimulated and this depended on co-operation not conflict: 'to get increased production there must be the closest possible co-operation between worker and capitalist.' The contents of a speech he made to motor manufacturers in November 1919, prompted iron and steel manufacturer J. F. Melling to write to Roberts: 'I, as an absolute Conservative, would be prepared to follow your lead or go with you anywhere at any time'.[76]

In September 1919 nearly half a million railway men went on strike. Clynes later recalled: 'troops in tin hats and with fixed bayonets guarded the main railway lines, food convoys of Army lorries were escorted by tanks and armoured cars, and every endeavour was made in certain quarters to give the struggle the character of revolution'.[77]

*The commemoration in Norwich of the final peace with Germany, 19 July 1919: Roberts on the balcony, towards the right.*

This was a crisis for Roberts, and one to which, at least in the eyes of the right-wing *Daily Telegraph*, he responded magnificently, he did not pose as a strike breaker, but saw that the public were fed: 'those arduous days provided Mr Roberts with his most conspicuous triumph. With all the railways paralysed, with food supplies concentrated in great masses, the organisation of the Food Controller contrived so efficient a system of emergency transport that no household lacked the necessaries or even the wonted luxuries of life. That piece of work is a title to national gratitude.' Preparations made by Roberts' ministry before the strike broke out swung into action. The country was divided into sixteen districts and 25,000 lorries requisitioned to distribute food. The requisitions were possible under the wartime Defence of the Realm Act, which was still in force; all that was necessary was for the Food Controller to declare that the situation was an 'Emergency'. The strike was settled in the first week of October.

This was a high point in Roberts' career. He was a successful member of a government in which he mixed with ex-Labour colleagues (George Barnes), Liberals (Lloyd George and Churchill), but which was dominated by Conservatives (Bonar Law, Balfour, Austen Chamberlain and many others). These great men were now his friends, and Roberts was also associating with European leaders. When M. Poincaré, the President of France, visited London in November 1919, he met many leading ministers, including Roberts. According to *The Times*, Poincaré welcomed Roberts 'with particular warmth': they had met in France three years earlier.

In the winter of 1919-1920, Roberts had another success, albeit on a minor scale. He managed to fix the winter price of milk at one shilling a quart, rather than the 1s. 3d. that the Ministry of Agriculture wanted. This must have pleased the consumers, but at the expense of Roberts' old friends the farming community. He was in Cabinet again on 28 December 1919 to report on the financial effects of the transactions

PUNCH, OR THE LONDON CHARIVARI.—October 15, 1919.

THE CHIEF OF THE STAFF OF LIFE.

MR. PUNCH (*decorating the* FOOD-CONTROLLER *for his admirable organisation during the strike*). "I AM TO SAY, SIR, THAT THE NATION THANKS YOU FROM THE BOTTOM OF ITS STOMACH."

*Punch, October 1919. Roberts is congratulated on his work as Minister of Food.*

of his Ministry. There was also a discussion on meat supply and the possibility of moving towards decontrol. Roberts must have seen the end of his role as Food Minister on the horizon.

In any event the role of ex-Labour men in the Coalition Government had run its course. When George Barnes resigned in January 1920, Roberts followed his lead. He resigned as Minister of Food in February: The *Daily Sketch* got wind of it in time for its 5 February edition, all other papers carrying the story on the following day. The precise reason for his resignation was never made clear. Barnes recalled:

> George followed me in a spirit of comradeship, and probably thinking as I did, that, having done our bit, we should go our way. There had been no more consistent supporter of the war policy than Mr Roberts ever since the dark days of August 1914, and few who had dared so much in giving expression to his views.[78]

Private letters from Barnes to Roberts flesh out the story. Barnes wrote to Roberts from a hotel in Falmouth on 21 January to let him know he had decided to resign from the government. It was because he no longer felt he was making a useful contribution: 'for me to hang on drawing a big screw for doing odd jobs would be a fraud on the public purse. And I don't want other entanglements. I shall therefore put in my resignation on getting home.' He made it clear he had no opinion on whether Roberts stayed on or not, and concluded: 'Whatever may happen to either of us we shall have the satisfaction of knowing that we stood by the Tommies who were suffering and by the country in the time of its greatest danger.' A week later, he wrote again to tell Roberts he had written to Lloyd George with his resignation, but did not know how the Press had got hold of the story, and reiterating his reasons: 'As you know my position was getting a public scandal. I had been sending Press cuttings commenting upon it, and I could not go on any longer.'[79]

As we have seen, Roberts had been reluctant to take the job on in the first place. He himself had said that the Food Ministry would be coming to an end in August 1920, as there would be no need of controls by then.* Roberts had been reported as saying in January that 'he was not quite satisfied with his position and with things generally', and the *Daily Sketch* thought that he had been overruled in his opposition to a recent measure of food decontrol. The *Daily Telegraph* noted that Roberts 'held very different views on profiteering and the method of tackling it from Sir Auckland Geddes and the dominant party in the Cabinet'.

The *Eastern Evening News* carried an interview with Roberts on 6 February, in which he told the reporter that he had actually handed in his resignation a week earlier but the announcement had been delayed as Lloyd George had asked him to reconsider. He added, 'the state of my health is really one of the reasons why my resignation has followed so closely on that of my friend Barnes ... I am advised that I must take a rest ... I have been trying to arrange for a holiday but the duties of the office are so exacting as to make it impossible. I had a big breakdown in 1912 and I was then advised to be very careful lest there should be a recurrence of it'.

It is hard to judge the success of Roberts' ministerial career. Much of the work in which he was involved was intentionally short term, dealing with difficulties arising from the war and from the crises immediately following it. As we have seen, his fellow ministers praised his hard work and ability to get things done, but inevitably former colleagues in the Labour Party, now his most bitter enemies,

---

* In fact, it lingered on as a separate department until March 1921 when it was dissolved, its few remaining responsibilities being taken over by the Board of Trade.

took every opportunity to denigrate his work. The Governments in which he was involved produced three pieces of legislation that changed the lives of many people in Britain. These were in the fields of suffrage, housing and unemployment.

The *Representation of the People Act (1918)* gave the vote to all men over twenty-one and, for the first time, to women, albeit only to those over thirty. Roberts was, as we have seen, in favour of giving women the vote, and, although he did not speak in the debate, he voted for the Bill in the crucial debate in the Commons on 19 June 1917.

The *Housing and Town Planning Act (1919)* provided subsidies for local authorities to build new homes, the 'Homes fit for Heroes' of which

*Roberts in a studio portrait.*

Lloyd George had spoken in the 1918 general election campaign. Roberts' own constituency, Norwich, led the way, starting with new housing estates at Angel Road and Mile Cross, followed by many others. Eventually, the city had a higher proportion of its inhabitants in council-owned housing than anywhere else in Britain. Equally important, many small towns and villages also began to build council houses, helping alleviate conditions for Roberts' beloved agricultural labourers.

The *Unemployed Insurance Act (1920)* effectively gave outdoor relief to many (not all) classes of unemployed, replacing the old Poor Law system with a hand-out, known ever since as the 'dole'. In the debate on this, Roberts, as he had done all his life, put forward the case for involving Friendly Societies. He said wryly, 'I am assured that in the next election I shall not receive much support from the organised Labour forces in Norwich. Therefore I ought to be currying favour with the great trade union movement...' Instead, he returned to a favourite theme of his, 'class antagonism', which he thought the new law would exacerbate. He thought Friendly Societies, where both employers and employees were members, would be better placed to help an unemployed man find new work in his profession, rather than just hand out 'dole'. When he sat down, another MP,

Lt-Col Croft, commented: 'His speech appeared to me to be absolutely candid and frank, and, as his speeches always are, full of courage.' After sixteen years in Parliament, and six as a minister, Roberts was still his own man, still ready to 'do different' as Norfolk people say.

Rumours inevitably abounded. Some people thought he might get another Government job. Others thought he might return to the Labour Party, but they were completely wrong: Roberts was no longer a Labour Party man. There were also rumours he might move to a constituency more favourable to his ideas the director of the *Acton District Post* wrote to Roberts asking if he was about to become Acton's next Member of Parliament.[80]

Roberts was right to think that some Labour men welcomed the new regime in Russia as an example that Britain might follow. George Lansbury visited Russia in February 1920 and brought back a message from Lenin himself, which he read out at the Albert Hall on 22 March: 'if you can bring about peaceful revolution in England, no one will be better pleased than we in Russia. Don't divide until you have to divide. Don't become disintegrated by premature strikes or premature upheavals. Keep together until you are homogeneous and do not be led into resorting to violence'.[81]

Roberts' move to the right was well illustrated in a speech he gave in the Commons on 16 February 1921. He said that many trade unionists were now unwilling to co-operate with employers: they had become infected with 'this Marxian or class war theory.' Many people become more 'conservative' as they get older, but for a I.L.P. man this was a dramatic turn around.

Roberts' career as a minister was over. However, as for so many ex-ministers, there were many other opportunities. As an MP, he developed his concern for the blind, speaking in a debate on provisions for the Blind in the House of Commons in June 1920, criticising the lack of generosity of the provisions, and stressing his role as an independent thinker:

> I am not speaking in any party sense, because I have frequently endeavoured throughout my professional life to lift the question of the blind above party ... While I am often criticised for being a perhaps too ready follower of the Government, that is not my concern ... I say that if the Government withdraw these proposals and submit something on a more generous scale, they will meet with the approval of the inhabitants of this country and the Members of this House.

In April 1921, the Minister of Health, Alfred Mond, set up an Advisory Committee on matters relating to the blind. Roberts was appointed Chairman

In March 1922 a proposal came before Parliament to cut spending on the blind from £100,000 to £80,000. Roberts protested:

> If they were going to put an end to or arrest the work that was now being done amongst the blind it would prove to be a false economy, and a most inhumane thing to do… As chairman of the committee investigating blindness he could say that it had been ascertained that a good deal of it was preventable, and he strongly urged that there should be no cessation of ameliorative work amongst children and the mentally defective.

The committee's report came out in October 1922, and Mond congratulated Roberts on his work.

Roberts also remained active, raising individual cases that concerned him. In July 1920, Roberts raised in Parliament the case of Matthew Lowe, a soldier who had deserted when his battalion was called into the front line on the Western Front in October 1918. He had deserted before, four months earlier, and for his second offence was sentenced to ten years penal servitude. Several MPs were uneasy: there were medical issues in the case, as well as the general question of whether deserters should still be held in prison now that the war was over. Winston Churchill, in his role as Secretary for War, pointed out that Lowe had already been told that he would be released not later than 20 November 1920, and he saw no need to change this. Roberts continued to see himself as very much a Norwich man, and was present in April 1921 when the Norwich Castle Museum launched an exhibition to celebrate the centenary of local artist John Crome.

Roberts, like many ex-ministers, also entered the business world. The directors of Coleman and Co. of Norwich, where he had worked as a young man, offered him a place on the Board, which he accepted. The offer came in a letter of 2 February 1920, when Roberts' resignation was rumoured but had not been formally announced. The firm's best known product was the tonic drink Wincarnis - 'recommended by thousands of Medical Men' according to their headed notepaper. Roberts' opponents were to remember this during his later election campaigns. He took up directorships, going on the board of Home Grown Sugar Ltd: and the development of the sugar beet industry in England became one of his greatest concerns.

Roberts remained no stranger to controversy. He was a strong supporter of birth control. He chaired a meeting in support of Marie Stopes at Queen's Hall, London, in May 1921. Stopes was the leading family planning campaigner of her day, writing books like *Married Life* (1918) and *A Letter to Working Mothers* (1919) in favour of the cause. Roberts said:

> I want to say, as one who has been identified with the working-class movement throughout the whole of my adult life, I am aware of the fact that well-to-do classes have the benefit of knowledge on this subject, and I desire that women of my own class shall be as adequately informed and intelligently equipped as the women in any other class of society. It is a deplorable fact today that while the better-to-do possess this knowledge, and are, in my opinion, ordering their lives so as to give children greater and fairer opportunities, the class to which I belong, grovelling in their ignorance, are still producing in excessive numbers, and producing a race which is not fitted for the Empire which we have to govern.

He went further, supporting Marie Stopes in her 1923 libel case. In 1921, she had opened a birth control clinic in Holloway, a working class part of North London. In 1922, Halliday Sutherland, a doctor and convert to Roman Catholicism, wrote about 'a doctor of German philosophy' who was giving pernicious advice to women in a clinic in a London slum. Stopes sued him for libel. Roberts gave evidence in support of Stopes. He was introduced as a former minister, a Privy Councillor and a Justice of the Peace. As an experienced politician, he was very comfortable in the witness box.

Question: Have you, in the course of your professional career, come across a large number of the poorer members of the community?
Roberts: Having lived with them all my life, I know them intimately.

Question: Do you remember pages of *Married Love* devoted to a minute description of the act of intercourse?
Roberts: I do.

Question: Do you think it advisable that a fully-sexed girl of 16 years old should buy and read this book?
Roberts: I think it far better that a girl should read from a wholesome book than obtain this information by surreptitious methods.

Roberts said that he thought a girl of sixteen should be educated in these matters. He was in favour of the widest possible dissemination of family planning information among young women and men before marriage. He praised two of Stopes' books that he had read, *Married Love* and *Wise Parenthood*, and thought they discussed their subject with delicacy and tact. He compared them favourably with some contemporary novels and their descriptions of sexual acts, which he found tasteless in their method of expression, but he freely admitted this was a matter of opinion. When asked if he had read her *A New Gospel to all Peoples*, he caused laughter in the courtroom by replying: 'I have it in reserve for a holiday recreation'. His long answers seem to have annoyed the counsel. At one point, he was asked impatiently, 'Cannot you answer 'Yes' or 'No'? Roberts replied calmly, 'In my political experience I have learned to answer in my own way and not as my opponent wants'.

*George Roberts talking to Marie Stopes the palaeobotanist and family planning pioneer.*

The jury found Sutherland's remarks true but defamatory and recommended that damages be awarded against him. However, the judge was hostile to Stopes throughout the trial and awarded judgement with costs to Sutherland.[82]

## The 1922 General Election

In 1922 Lloyd George planned to fight another general election under the Coalition banner. Although Conservative ministers accepted this, their backbenchers rebelled and resolved to fight as an independent party. Lloyd George could not continue as Prime Minister without them. He resigned at once. The Conservative leader, Andrew Bonar Law became Prime Minister and formed a cabinet. However, the Conservatives who had been in Lloyd George's cabinet, such as Arthur Balfour and Austen Chamberlain, would not join. The cabinet had to be made up of largely unknown figures. Bonar Law called an election. During it he promised that the government would not introduce Protection without calling a further election specifically on the 'Protection or Free Trade' issue.

The election following the collapse of Lloyd George's coalition was held in November 1922. Roberts, of course, could not stand for Labour. They regarded him as a traitor to their cause and put up two candidates in Norwich, Witard and George Johnson. Roberts had no party support, so he took a bold step. He would stand as an Independent and trust that the people of Norwich would support him as an individual, rather than as a member of any political party. His actual candidature was as a 'Lloyd George' Liberal, as opposed to being an official

Liberal candidate. *The Times* summed up his position:

> Having wound up Food Control in 1920, he continued to support
> the Coalition as an unofficial member, still styling himself 'Labour'
> but moving far from the Labour Party to the Right. Rumour has it
> that he will come out as an Independent, relying on his prestige as a
> Norwich man and his services in Parliament and having as a
> slogan 'Down with Socialism and up with trade and employment.'[83]

Hilton Young stood once more for the Liberals. He said that he would support any government in resisting, to the last, Socialistic and revolutionary proposals. Earlier in the year he had married Kathleen Scott. She was the widow of Robert Falcon Scott, the explorer who had died so tragically on his return from the South Pole in 1912.

Roberts' impact in the city was so great that others tried to hang on to his coat tails. The local elections of 1922 were actually held during the Parliamentary campaign. Walter Barnes had been elected three years earlier for Labour. Now, standing for re-election as an Independent candidate, he stressed that he was Roberts' election agent and stated:

> On this occasion I offer myself as an Independent Progressive, my
> three years on the Council have convinced me that the administration
> of local affairs is above party politics, and that service to the citizens
> stands first. I am therefore standing absolutely free of all political
> parties.

It must have been seen as a bad omen for Roberts when Barnes was trounced. He received 310 votes with his only opponent, the Liberal candidate C. F. Watling, getting 1,134 votes.

The Labour Election Finance Committee issued an open letter in October, urging a return to politics of principle:

> The Labour Party ... has ideals of human brotherhood, of justice
> between man and man, of an enhanced value and fullness of life
> for all of us: ideals which we intend to put into practice when the
> time comes. We therefore call for help to every man and woman to
> whom honour and freedom, mercy and straight dealing (all set at
> nought by the Coalition) are living springs of conduct, and not mere
> names. In Norwich we have two excellent candidates, men of affairs,
> well known and trusted for many years in the Labour and Socialist
> Movement, men of intense conviction, courage and capacity.

Roberts' own election address reminded the electors that in 1918 he had said that the problems caused by the war were so great that they could only be dealt with 'by the co-operation of all men and women willing to place national interests before those of party'. He thought this was still the case.

> Being still convinced of the desirability of maintaining the largest possible measure of national unity, I shall be prepared, if re-elected, to support the new Government in steps proved necessary to the re-settlement of Europe, to promote harmonious relationships with all countries, to secure the prosperity of trade and commerce, and to provide wise solutions of the social and economic problems that beset the country. In so doing I shall feel the trust reposed in me is being properly discharged by exercising the freedom to associate with any other party or section, animated by national and not party considerations, in offering helpful and constructive criticism on specific questions.

He concluded with an appeal to his record.

> This is the seventh time I have solicited the support of the Electors of the City in a Parliamentary Election. Now I do so in the belief that, judged in broad survey, my record proves I have carried out my duties faithfully and efficiently. Also that service in various Ministerial capacities has given me knowledge and experience which enhance my ability to serve the constituency and the country.

One sign of change is that his occupation in the nomination papers was given as 'Company Director': in 1918, it had been 'Organiser, Typographical Association'.

As an Independent, Roberts had no party organisation behind him. On 3 November he hired St Andrew's Hall at his own expense. The hall was crowded. As Roberts spoke he was frequently interrupted by bursts of 'The Red Flag' and 'Tell Me the Old Old Story'. He urged people to vote for him and Young. When a heckler called out 'What are you?' Roberts retorted: 'I am a decent honest chap, one who is not afraid of changing his opinion, and when he has so changed of coming out and telling people why he has done it'. As 'The Red Flag' broke out again, Roberts responded, 'I believe I could sing it better than you now (Laughter)'. He got into his stride:

> I am charged with changing my coat. If I find a better and cleaner one I will change it, and the conduct of those who are interrupting me tonight gives one indication why I preferred not to keep their company any longer (Cheers). I was brought up in the British sport and the British tradition to respect my opponents and honour my

*Roberts as statesman and politician: undated and unidentified images from his personal archive. Some are probably taken in Versailles, 1919.*

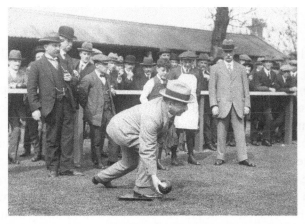

friends. You are exhibiting a quality that is foreign to the city of Norwich. We were always willing to hear our opponents.

The meeting ended with rival groups singing 'The Red Flag' and 'He's A Jolly Good Fellow'.

The Labour candidate, Herbert Witard, said that he had been Roberts lieutenant for over 25 years and did not think that he had a superabundance of knowledge of economics and social studies. However, Witard had his own past to defend, in his case his pacifism during the war. When a questioner asked him 'What did you do during the war?' he replied 'Well at least I did not do anybody else. Surely you will not ask me to denounce a crime and then take part in it'. Witard was probably thinking of a remark made by Mary Macarthur's husband, the anti war MP Willie Anderson. He referred to the famous poster of a child sitting on its father's knee and asking 'Daddy, what did YOU do in the Great War?' Anderson said that when any ship-owner's child asked that question, her father would have to reply 'I DID EVERYBODY'. The implication was clear: manufacturers took advantage of the war to amass enormous profits for themselves.

Roberts enjoyed the rough and tumble of campaigning. At one meeting he said: 'I like public life: I like the strife. This election has been a tonic to me already, and I feel more boyish than ever in my life'. At another meeting, he pointed out that it was the Coalition government in which he served that had carried through the enfranchisement of women. A heckler cried: 'A jolly good job for you'. Roberts, a lifelong supporter of woman's suffrage, responded at once 'Yes, I think the women are going to reflect the fact that they are really intelligent citizens (Applause)'.

Roberts and Hilton Young openly worked together against the two Labour Party candidates. Roberts brought Young on stage during his last meeting. Roberts' final words were 'With a long pull, a strong pull, and a pull together, and down will come the Socialist hooligans (Loud and continued cheers)'.

The result was a triumph for Roberts, his highest vote ever, and as a non-party man, a tribute to his personality and to his achievements as an MP over the previous sixteen years:

## General Election 1922:

| ROBERTS (Independent) | 31,167 |
|---|---|
| HILTON YOUNG (National Liberal) | 31,151 |
| Witard (Labour) | 15,609 |
| Johnson (Labour) | 14,490 |

No less than 29,474 people voted for both Roberts and Young, compared with 13,835 voting for the Witard-Johnson combination.

As an Independent, Roberts had technically nowhere to go to celebrate his victory, but Young took him to the Liberal Club, and to the Gladstone Club, of which he had been a member when he first entered politics three decades earlier. He was cheered loudly in both clubs. At the latter he said of Young: 'He has a greater future before him, but I am afraid I have got almost as far as I shall get. (Shouts of 'No')'.

In terms of votes, the country split three ways. The Conservatives got 5½ million votes, Labour and the Liberals a little over 4 million votes each. However, in terms of seats, the Conservatives won a majority of 77 over all the other parties combined. Labour won 142 seats, a gain of more than 80 over the previous election. It was the Liberals who suffered. They were split into two parties, the Lloyd George supporters (National Liberals) and the Independent Liberals who supported Asquith. They won just 117 seats, split roughly half and half between the rival factions. For the first time in history, Labour had overtaken the Liberals to become the official Opposition Party, but would it last?

Roberts sat in Parliament as an Independent for ten months. He was offered the National Liberal whip several times, but always refused it. Indeed he was in the habit of sitting with the Conservative members in the House of Commons. In April 1923, he made what was to be his last intervention in the House of Commons, querying the cost to taxpayers of money spent on the International Labour Organisation. Socialist MP Campbell Stephen congratulated Roberts on the way 'he has acquired the point of view, if not the accent, of members on the other side of the House ... we on this side of the House appreciate the manner in which he is now fulfilling his new role in life'.

Roberts completed his political journey to the right in August 1923 when he joined the Conservative Party! Why did he do this? He gave a typically honest answer: after sitting in the Commons as an Independent he realised that it 'was impossible to act as an individual'. So he looked at each party, deciding which one to join. First he thought about the Labour Party:

> A lengthy experience with the Labour Party made it impossible for me to entertain the idea of a return to that party. In fact, my main reason for remaining in politics is to assist in combating the new brand of Socialism now impressed on that party.

He had stinging words for his former friends in the Labour Party, arguing that times had changed since he was a member:

I have devoted a large portion of my life to the building up of a Labour party. In recent years this party has completely changed, and now stands for nearly everything I consider prejudicial to the common interests. We used to protest against the power exerted by feudal and other interests, but in many instances there could be no greater tyranny than that displayed by those who have manoeuvred themselves into the leadership against others who have ventured to claim reasonable liberty of thought and of actions. It was the habit to point to the victimisation practised by the lesser employers against the men who sought to protect their fellows. The new Labour party is as autocratic as any body that has previously existed, and deprives men of the means whereby they have earned their livelihood if they dare to take an independent line such as they believe to be in the interests of the community.

As we have seen, the Liberals were split into two parties, the Independents led by Asquith and the National Liberals, led by Lloyd George. Roberts rejected the Independents: 'they have exhibited a feverish desire not to offend the Labour Party'. He was more attracted to the Nationals, though mainly for personal reasons: 'one cannot forget the great service rendered to his country by Lloyd George throughout the war'. However, he thought 'the Liberal party is too broken up to be an effective barrier against Socialism'.

He had come to the conclusion that the most important issue was that of promoting trade and employment. In his view the Conservatives were the only party who could achieve this:

> To help to free my fellow trade unionists, to uphold the national constitution, to assist in restoring the trade of the world, and to help forward ordered progress and wise reform, objects which believe the party now in power is best designed and inspired to accomplish, are the reasons why I have decided to throw in my lot with the Conservative Party.[84]

It was the Conservatives alone who could combat the Socialism of Labour party 'extremists'.

Roberts formally joined the Conservative benches, one of a very small number of people to have served as a Labour MP, as an Independent and as a Conservative. One of his first local actions in his new role was to open the Ideal Home Exhibition at the Agricultural Hall in Norwich in November. He earned himself some favour locally by persuading the organisers to give 5% of the takings and a minimum sum of 50 guineas, to the Norfolk and Norwich Hospital.

Roberts did not have long to wait before putting his new-found convictions to the people of Norwich. Baldwin had decided in favour of tariff reform, but felt obliged to honour Bonar Law's pledge that this would not be introduced before a further general election was called. It was held on 6 December 1923. The Norwich Conservative Party was delighted to have such a famous recruit, and they immediately adopted him as one of their candidates.

# 5

# 'Sing us The Red Flag, Georgie': the 1923 General Election in Norwich

The 1923 election was an exceptional one for Norwich. They had two sittin MPs, who had been elected by large majorities against 'extreme' [that is, anti war] Labour candidates, one as a National Liberal, the other (Roberts) as a Independent, but closely associated with the National Liberals. Now everythin had changed. Roberts now stood for the Conservatives, in partnership with second Conservative candidate, Henry Swan. Swan was a former professiona cricketer for Essex: he had no connections with Norwich. Labour also turne to new faces as both 'extremists', Witard and Johnson, had decided not to stan again. They chose Walter Smith and Dorothy Jewson, both linked with the trad union movement. The Liberals already had one candidate in Hilton Young but he was now running in opposition to Roberts rather than with him. On 1 November they announced their second candidate, Henry Copeman, the head o a prominent firm of provision merchants, and leader of the Liberal party on th City Council.

This was the first time in history that each of the three parties had put up tw candidates in Norwich:. Each elector could cast their two votes for members o the same party, without having to make the usual decision as to whether to plum for their candidate or to cast their second vote for a candidate of a different party

Roberts and Swan put out a joint election leaflet. This was almost entirel about tariff control, supporting Conservative plans to put duties onto importe goods, and to give preference to products from Empire countries. Agricultur was also considered, with a proposal to give a bounty to farms who kept thei fields under plough: 'this is designed to maintain labour on the land and to kee up the wages of agricultural workers'. To ensure this the bounty would only b given to farmers who paid their labourers thirty shillings a week. This magi figure, which Roberts thought impossible to obtain seven years earlier, was no an election pledge.

The campaign was bitterly fought. On 16 November, there was a Conservativ meeting at St Andrew's Hall. Roberts announced that trades unions had allowe themselves to be captured by Socialists and Bolsheviks and 'to breathe the poison gas of the class war theory'. They had aggravated unemployment and so caused many women and children to want the necessaries and the amenities of life. He was cheered when he said that the Conservative Party represented the only chance of doing something for the agricultural labourer — 'the class from which he himself came.'

Roberts inevitably faced severe heckling at his meetings, to which he responded with cheerful and witty replies. As we have already seen, this was one of his great strengths — 'quick of mind and scorching in repartee, he was at his best when he had to face a roaring audience'.[85]

On 22 November, at a meeting at Cowgate Street School, he said that Baldwin had given him his word that there would be no tax on certain foodstuffs. A heckler called out 'What about Wincarnis?' which evoked a shout of laughter. Roberts had the crowd in fits of laughter when he retorted 'Thank you, my friend, for mentioning that. I hope others will do the same, for then people will enquire all the more into its virtues'.

Roberts' Socialist past came back to haunt him. At a meeting on 23 November at Bull Close Road School, Mr Maxey, as former secretary of the Norwich Labour Party, asked Roberts to reconcile his present attitude with his former statement that 'the squalor and misery from which the people are suffering today is due to the Capitalist system ... I will do all I can to break down such a form of society and substitute for it the Socialist Industrial Commonwealth'. Roberts agreed that had once been his opinion 'but I have never denied that I have fundamentally altered my opinion (A loud 'Ah' came from the audience). I have done so and given my reasons for it. You have no complaint on that score. I regard myself in this election as good a labour man as there is in this country'. Maxey pointed out that he himself had written the letter expelling Roberts from the Labour Party. On the same day, Dorothy Jewson spoke at the Avenue Road School. The chairman reminded her audience that she and her brother had done splendid work in exposing flaws in the administration of the Poor Law system in Norwich. Dorothy said that she had been visiting the poorer parts of the Wensum ward and was astonished by the housing conditions — far worse than before the war.[86]

At a meeting at Thorpe Hamlet Boys' School on 26 November, Roberts seemed to admit the possibility of defeat. He said that he hoped that people would remember that even a Socialist Government would have to introduce Protection to help British workers. To laughter, he added that he had found that his Socialist friends were just as keen on scenting a little profit for themselves as any other members of the community.

Further heckling followed. At Philadelphia Girls' School on 27 November,

*The six candidates for the two Norwich seats, 1923.*

Roberts was talking about agriculture. A heckler caused laughter when he asked 'Didn't you tell the men in the St Faiths strike to fight hard against the side you are now advocating? Roberts replied that he was quite ready to fight for the agricultural labourer. At Nelson Street School on the following day, he was asked whether he had joined the Tory Party because he expected that 'in the next shuffle you will get a job in the Cabinet with a good screw'. Roberts pledged that he would not take any Government position. At the end of another meeting, someone called out - 'Sing us the Red Flag before you go, George!'

Although Roberts was heckled far more than the other candidates, others suffered too. At Heigham School on the 28th, Young was heckled so badly that he had to sit down without making his speech.

The arguments surfaced in letters to the press as well. On 28 November, Walter Rye, antiquarian and former Mayor of Norwich, published a letter in the *Eastern Daily Press* saying that, after having voted Tory all his life, he was now supporting Hilton Young because he had fought gallantly in the war and lost an arm. Avelyn Deane, writing from Tunstead Vicarage, responded, 'May I remind the women of Norwich of the work during the war of Mr Roberts as Food Controller. He did not lose an arm, certainly, but helped us to keep our babies alive. We in the country remember'.

The biggest name to come to Norwich was Lloyd George, speaking for the Liberal candidates. He addressed a sell-out crowd at the Hippodrome. There was so much demand that an overflow meeting was held at the Haymarket Picture House. The speeches were relayed there, and Lloyd George also called in after the Hippodrome meeting finished. Lloyd George reminded his listeners of Hilton Young's war record. He compared Young to another Norfolk hero who had lost an arm in battle, Admiral Nelson. He did not mention his former cabinet colleague, George Roberts.

Roberts replied on the following day, saying that Lloyd George had played a great part in the war. He was one of the finest platform orators in the world, but they needed more than flowing words today.

*The Times* of 30 November carried a report on Norwich suggesting that there might be a split result: 'as the candidates are in pairs the race is more like a chariot race than a horse race ... [however] it may happen that one of the riders from two of the competing chariots may win — each, as it were, jumping from his car and by his personal merits reaching the winning-post on foot'. Clearly the paper was thinking that the personalities of Roberts and Young might propel them to success, even if there were swings against the parties for which they were standing.

In fact, both men were defeated:

## General Election 1923:

| SMITH (Labour) | 20,077 |
|---|---|
| JEWSON (Labour) | 19,304 |
| Young (Liberal) | 16,222 |
| Roberts (Conservative) | 14,749 |
| Copeman (Liberal) | 13,180 |
| Swan (Conservative) | 12,713 |

The turnout was 79.7%, compared with 78.5% in the previous election in 1922.

Most people voted for the two candidates from their favoured party, but there was also all sorts of cross voting, and also 'plumping' — where a voter deliberately cast only one of the two votes he was allowed. These figures were published with the results. 18,588 people voted for both Labour candidates, 12,765 for both Liberal candidates, and 12,112 for both Conservative candidates. The greatest number of cross-voters by a long way were those favouring the two sitting MPs. Roberts and Young — 1,867 people went for this combination. As a result Roberts polled over 2,000 more votes than his Conservative ally: his magic still held for *some* city voters.

Roberts admitted that from the result it might be imputed that something was lacking on the part of one or both the Conservative candidates. Swan felt that he might have been a millstone about Roberts' neck because he was not a local man. He went out of his way to say that Roberts 'had stuck to him in a way he should never forget'.

# 6

# 'Never afraid to say what was on his mind' – the last years of George Roberts

Roberts lived in Cardiff Road when he was first elected, moving to 22, Whitehall Road by 1908 and 42, Whitehall Road by 1916. In later life, and certainly by 1922, he lived at 104, Earlham Road. He named it 'Westminster House', a name it still carried on its gate-post almost four decades after his death.[87]

After losing his seat, Roberts expanded his career as businessman. In April 1924 he spoke at a meeting of the British Sugar Beet Society where he said that the British could grow sugar beet as well as any other country: 'with more factories they could produce all the beet required'. He could not resist making a political point on his favourite subject, agriculture. He thought that whatever party was in power, it would soon have to foster agriculture: 'the longer this was deferred the more costly it would be to the State'. He returned to the theme in the following month, recalling the shortage of sugar during the war and commenting that Britain must produce more of its food requirements at home.[88]

By the time of the 1924 general election, Roberts was already much more interested in pushing forward his business interests than he was in politics. On 5 November he attended a Smoke Abatement League Conference in Manchester. He had a product to sell them – Coalite. This was made by a firm of which he happened to be a director, Low Temperature Carbonisation Limited. He claimed that London coal merchants were ordering up all the Coalite that the firm could produce. According to Roberts, the product met the British demand for an open fire and yet, unlike coke, was completely smokeless: 'It lights as easily as coke and it burns without smell and produces a cheerful fire. Just like coal at its best'. Roberts' oratory was now being used to sell, rather than in a political cause. However, he failed to convince the League, who thought that people would continue to burn coal as long as it was cheaper than smokeless fuels.[89]

Roberts had many other business interests, becoming chairman of Hecate Burner Co. and of Westminster Advertising Services, and director of the Scholes Construction Co., in addition to those already mentioned. The latter connection recalls the remark of Stanley Baldwin about the 1918 House of Commons being made up of hard-faced men who had done well out of the war. Roberts' dealings with Scholey had begun in joint meetings in 1917 of the Industrial League for the Improvement of Relations between Employers and Employed. He had evidently corresponded with Scholey when he was still Minister of Food. Scholey had written to Roberts on the day his resignation was announced, (6 February 1920), saying that he was interested to hear the news, 'which is of course what you have contemplated doing for some time past'. He offered Roberts a place on the Board, which he accepted. Another of his interests was the Northern Exploration Company.

The Conservative Party still saw him as a potential MP for their cause. In October 1926, Sir Herbert Blain wrote to him from Conservative Central Office referring to a Lancashire constituency that was looking 'for a man of your type', adding: 'there are many who would like to see you back in the House'. Roberts refused to bite. In any case, he had heart problems in these final years. He was in a poor state in the early months of 1926. The Sporting Times of 27 March referring to a recently-held supper, said of Roberts, 'happily recovered from his recent severe illness, [he] was early on the scene, complete with big carnation and ditto cigar.'

Roberts recovered sufficiently to spend the summer of 1926 on an extensive business tour of Canada and the United States. A Canadian newspaper described him as one of the outstanding men in the ranks of British labor' and noted that he had 'held some of the highest offices yet attained by a member of the Labor party of Great Britain.' This was just after the General Strike in Britain, and he told his Canadian audience that there would be no more general strikes as the British worker did not believe in 'red revolution' but in law and order and constitutional rights. He was cynical about his former socialist colleagues: 'Whenever I hear Socialists speaking loftily of the brotherhood of man, I look at the advocate and I find that he is as full of shortcomings as the ones he criticises'.

He was now chairman of the Committee of Management of the British Sugar Beet Society. This was a profitable business, rapidly expanding in the 1920s. At a triumphant Annual General Meeting in 1926, Roberts was able to boast that the acreage under sugar beet in the country had grown from 22,000 acres to 128,000 acres in the previous two years, and the number of factories processing the crop had risen from just three to ten in the same period. There were three sugar beet factories in England by 1925, including the first one at Cantley, Norfolk. Four more were opened in the summer of 1925. As Chairman, Roberts met with the Management Committee of the General Federation of Trade Unions at the newly-opened factory at Ipswich in November. The Times noted that the factory had been begun in March and had cost over £400,000 and that the union leaders were impressed with the state-of-the-art technology.[90]

Roberts wrote to the Prime Minister, Stanley Baldwin, about some unspecified aspect of the industry: the reply survives from Baldwin written in December 1926 noting Roberts' 'support for Alfred Wood's claim to recognition'. Wood was the Secretary of the British Sugar Beet Society, and had just announced his resignation due to pressure of other duties: no doubt Roberts had suggested some kind of honour for him.[91]

*Roberts opening the Ideal Home exhibition in Norwich, 1924.*

Roberts continued to be concerned with the care of the blind even after he had left Parliament. He continued as Chairman of the Advisory Committee on the welfare of the blind. John Wheatley, Minister of Health, in the 1923 Labour Government was a 'Red Clydesider' and must have been wholly opposed to Roberts' political views. However, he wrote to Roberts thanking him 'for the very able and conscientious manner in which you have presided over the committee and for the privilege of your assistance in dealing with the problem of the Blind when so many demands upon your services have been made in other directions.' He continued as Chairman under the succeeding Conservative government, and, as late as 29 December 1927, he was re-appointed Chairman. It was to be his last appointment.

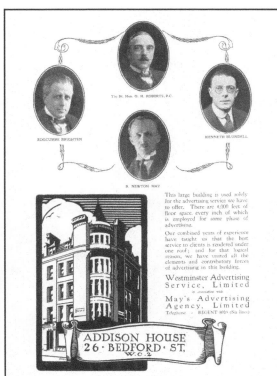

In April 1928, the vote was extended to include all men and women over the age of 21. The result of the vote in Parliament was 387 in favour, with just ten voting against. Emmeline Pankhurst was present to see the final consummation of her lifelong campaign. Roberts also approved. However much his political opinions had changed in his lifetime, he had remained a committed supporter of universal suffrage. In fact it was to be the last political change he was to see as he was taken ill

*Roberts in Montreal, Canada, May 1926.*

*After his defeat, Roberts developed many business interests.*

later in the month. He died from heart failure on 25 April at Edenhurst, Sevenoaks, a hotel where he had been staying on his doctor's advice. He was 59 years old.

After his death, T. P. O'Connor wrote: 'Georgie — as he was invariably called — always looked, and to a certain extent always remained, a boy. The short stature, the chubby cheeks, the very bright and striking eyes, the soft manner, they all suggested one of the Peter Pans of political

life'. A local paper summed up his character: 'quick of mind and scorching in repartee, he was at his best when he had to face a roaring audience, as he often had to do.'[92]

By chance, there was a meeting of the Junior Imperial League in Norwich on 27 April, and fulsome tributes were paid. The chairman described Roberts as 'one who certainly showed energy, enthusiasm and determination to do whatever he could for the people among whom he resided'. The Air Minister, Samuel Hoare, was at the meeting. He too praised Roberts: 'a man who was never afraid to say what was in his mind and admit a change of opinion if he thought the time had come to change'. A unique character, it comes as no surprise to find that in 1918 he was appointed Honorary Life Member of the Eccentric Club![93]

*Roberts in later life.*

*Roberts' grave in Earlham Road cemetery, 1928.*

*George and Annie Roberts' grave, sadly neglected until restored in 2018.*

After a funeral service at St Thomas' church on the Earlham Road, Roberts was buried at Earlham Road Cemetery, Norwich on 30 April 1928. As he died a Conservative, his old Labour colleagues were not well represented at his funeral. Since Roberts was an honorary freeman, Herbert Witard had to be there, in his capacity as Lord Mayor of the city — the first Labour Party mayor of Norwich in fact. Roberts died without leaving a will. His estate was valued at £7,110 (£1,514 net). Annie, his wife, died in April 1944, aged 70. Her place of residence at the time was 235 College Road. She is buried with her husband. Their grave was for many years neglected and its inscriptions indecipherable. George Roberts has been largely forgotten in Norwich. As the city's first Socialist MP, and as a successful Cabinet minister, 'Our Georgie' deserves to be remembered.

# Endnotes

1    The *Dictionary of Labour Biography* is the only near-contemporary source to state that he was actually born in 1868. I have checked the General Register Office (GRO) indexes and can confirm that 1868 is correct. The *Who's Who in Norfolk* (1912) gives the false date of 1869 — and the entries in this publication were presumably written by the entrants themselves.

2    Norfolk Record Office (hereafter NRO), PD 604/2

3    1871 census returns, 1822/42/21. The previous family recorded in the census is made up of George Roberts and his wife Elizabeth, almost certainly the grandparents of our George Roberts.    This George is described as a shoe clicker (the person who cuts the uppers for boots or shoes from a skin of leather). Perhaps the family were living with him until they found their own accommodation in the city.

4    NRO, Earlham cemetery registers.   I searched the registers between 1869 and 1881 and found no other siblings. The name Roberts is very common of course, which makes a search of the GRO indexes of births and deaths for these children an impractical one.

5    NRO, N/ED 1/75; N/ED 8/64

6    *Eastern Daily Press* (hereafter *E.D.P.*) 26 April 1928. This newspaper has been used as the main source for Norwich events.   I only cite it when the date of an entry is not obvious, as here.   In other cases the reference is to the newspaper of the day following the event described. The newspaper was not published on Sunday, so that Saturday's happenings appear in the paper for the following Monday.   The choir reference is from *The Church Family Newspaper* 24 August 1917

7    Cherry, Steven (1989) *Doing Different? Politics and the Labour Movement in Norwich 1880-1914* pp. 51-2; NRO, SO 198/7 [the Trades Council minute book]

8    Hawkins, C. B. (1910) *Norwich, A Social Study* p 278

9    Ancient Order of Foresters, High Court Meeting, *Guide to Norwich*, 1897

10   *Daylight* Annual 1905 p 157

11   Shepherd, John (2002) *George Lansbury* p 84

12   *Norfolk Socialist Review*, May 1901, NRO, SO 198/5/52/7

13   Clynes, J. R. (1937) *Memoirs 1869-1924* p 76

14   T.U.C. Conference Report 1894; Benn, Caroline (1992) *Keir Hardie* p 120

15   Hawkins, *op. cit.* p 99

16   *E.D.P.* 18 October 1894

17   *Daylight* 27 October 1894

18 *Daylight* 21 November 1896
19 *Daylight* 7 November 1896
20 *Daylight* Annual 1897 p 106
21 *Pearson's Weekly* 17 May 1906
22 *E.D.P.* 28 March 1928
23 *E.D.P.* 28 March 1928
24 NRO, HEN 43/86 25 NRO, SO 248/2/1/1
26 Hamilton, Mary (1938) *Arthur Henderson* p 58
27 *Daylight* Annual 1905 p 115, 116
28 T.U.C. Report 1904
29 NRO, N/TC 1/48, 49, 72
30 *Norwich Elector*, September 1906
31 *Norwich Elector*, March 1905
32 *Norwich Elector*, December 1905, January 1906
33 *E.D.P.* 6 December 1905, quoted in *Norwich Elector* December 1905
34 Weir, L. M. *The Tragedy of Ramsay MacDonald* (1938) p 37, 39
35 *Daylight* Annual 1908 p 107
36 *E.D.P.* 25 April 1928, quoting from Pearson's Weekly 17 May 1906
37 *Lloyd's Sunday News*, 15 June 1919.
38 NRO, MC 655/1; Morgan, Kenneth *Keir Hardie* (1975) p 155
39 *Hansard* 1906; Hawkins op cit p 165
40 Newton, Douglas (1985) *British Labour, European Socialism and the struggle for peace 1889-1914*, passim
41 Cherry, Steven op. cit. p. 57
42 *Daylight* Annual 1910, p 46
43 T.U.C. Report 1911
44 T.U.C. Report 1913; Roberts mentions the Denmark visit in a speech in Parliament, 25 February 1915. Ellis, Peter Berresford (1987 edn) *H Rider Haggard, a voice from the infinite* pp 188-9
45 *The Suffragette* 7 February 1913
46 *The Times* 23-31 October 1912
47 Newton, op. cit. p 238
48 Newton, op. cit. p 302
49 *E.D.P.* 30 June 1913
50 *E.D.P.* 9 July 1913
51 NRO, MC 655/47; SO 198/7/1
52 *The Times* 6 February 1920
53 T.U.C. Report 1915
54 Pugh, Martin (2011 edn), *Speak for Britain* p 115
55 NRO, MC 655/6: Roberts' copy of the minutes and reports of the Commission.
56 NRO, MC 655/29
57 NRO, MC 655/15
58 *Daily Herald* 5 Feb 1916
59 *Daily Herald* 5 July 1916

60  *Daily Herald* 16 December 1915
61  NRO, MC 655/14
62  Marquand, David *Ramsay MacDonald* (1977) pp 212-215; Hamilton, Mary *Arthur Henderson* (1938) p 123; Wrigley, Chris *Lloyd George and the British Labour Movement* (1976) p 208
63  *The Times*, 18 August 1917; NRO, MC 655/8
64  *The Times*, 29 August 1917
65  The new *Oxford Dictionary of National Biography* says that Roberts left the I.L.P. in 1914. My information comes from original letters at the Norfolk Record Office. (NRO, MC 655).
66  NRO, MC 655/7,14
67  Wrigley op. cit. pp 228, 230
68  NRO, MC 655/8
69  Banger, Joan *Norwich at Peace* (Poppyland Publishing 2003) p 10
70  NRO, MC 655/8
71  NRO, MC 655/8: letter from Lloyd George to Roberts offering him the post, 9 January 1919; Roberts' letter of refusal, 10 January 1919
72  *The Times* 13 January 1919
73  *The Future*
74  NRO, MC 655/8
75  E.D.P. 2 April 1919
76  NRO, MC 655/7
77  Barnes, George *From Workshop to War Cabinet* (1923) p 278
78  Barnes, George *From Workshop to War Cabinet* (1923) p 278
79  NRO, MC 655/15
80  NRO, MC 655/31: Roberts' own collection of news cuttings about his resignation; NRO, MC 655/7.
81  Shepherd op cit p 184
82  *Oxford Dictionary of National Biography* (2004 edition), Marie Stopes
83  *The Times* 25 October 1922
84  *Evening Standard* 2 August 1923
85  E.D.P. 26 April 1928
86  Dorothy's career is described in Frank Meeres, *Dorothy Jewson — Suffragette and Socialist* (Poppyland Publishing, 2014)
87  NRO, SO 198/5/52/13
88  *The Times* 10 April, 3 May 1924
89  *The Times* 6 November 1924
90  *The Times* 27 November 1925
91  NRO, MC 655/7
92  E.D.P. 26 April 1928
93  E.D.P. 28 April 1928; NRO, MC 655/10

# Index

Roman Catholic 16, 21
Runciman, Walter 60
Russia 61, 69, 80
Ruthin, George 44
Rye, Walter 94

St. Andrew's Hall 31
St. Benedict's 13
St. Faiths 37
St. Stephen's school 11
Scholey 97
    Scholey Construction Co 96
School Boards 10, 16, 19, 22-23, 31,
    37
school system 16
Seamen's and Fireman's Union 62
Sidney Henry 14
Smith, Walter 17, 23, 29, 92
Snowden, Philip 40
Social Democratic Federation (S.D.F.)
    17-18, 20, 22-23, 29
Socialist, Socialism 15, 17, 20, 22-24,
    29, 30, 35, 39, 49, 55, 61, 63-
    64, 84, 88-90, 93, 101-104
Socialist National Defence Committee
    55
Stanley, Arthur 62
Stephen, Campbell 89
Stockholm Conference 62
Stopes, Marie 81-83
suffrage 30, 38, 41, 42, 79, 88, 99
Sutherland, Halliday 82
Sutton, Alf 18, 21-22
Swan, Henry 92

soft drinks manufacture 13
Thurton 9-10
Tillett, Louis 34
Trade Boards Bill 35
Trades Union Congress (T.U.C.) 18,
    27, 39, 45, 54-55, 67, 102-103
Trades Union Movement 39
trades unions 14, 39, 64, 92
Tramways Company 13

Tribunal system 60
Tupper, 'Captain' 62
Typographical Association 13, 27, 30,
    63, 67, 85

unemployment 16, 31, 34, 39, 79, 93
Versailles, Conference 72, 74, 86
Watling, C. F. 84
weaving 15
Wheatley, John 98
Whellum, Walter 21
White, George 29
Wild, Ernest 26
Wilson, Joseph Havelock 17
Witard, Herbert 18, 23-24, 29-30, 54,
    63, 67, 69-70, 83, 88, 92, 101
Women's Social and Political Union 42
Wood, Alfred 98
Workhouse 16, 36

Young, Hilton 65, 69, 84